Greg

God is Able!

But am I Willing?

Dr. Greg T. Mathis

PRESS

God is Able!
But am I Willing?
by Dr. Greg T. Mathis

Printed in the United States of America

ISBN 978-1-60791-360-3

Cover photo by Collwyn Cleveland. Cover design by Jean Hefner. Photo of Dr. Mathis courtesy of Scott Hill.

www.xulonpress.com

Acknowledgements

I could not have written this book without the encouragement and help of the wonderful team around me. Probably not until we all get to Heaven will these incredible brothers and sisters in Christ know what they mean to me personally and to the ministry God has given us at Mud Creek Baptist Church. I sincerely appreciate the contribution of each one to this endeavor, *God is Able! But am I Willing?* I am indebted to my personal assistant, Susan Garrett, for her persistence in transcribing this entire book from a handwritten manuscript. I am grateful to Chris Roberts, Chris Hefner, and Sherri Hill for their help in editing and compilation. I am grateful to Jean Hefner for her editing and creativity in design of the cover for this book. I am indebted to my son, Jared Mathis, for his help in the editing process and for his contributions to the study questions for each chapter. I am also grateful to Mark Hunnicutt for his creative mind that has helped shape this book. I want to say a special word of thanks to my research assistant, Robert Hefner, for his management in the coordination, compilation, and completion of this project. Further, I cannot thank Sam Varner enough for helping begin this journey and guiding me at so many points along the way. Most of all, I would offer praise and thanks to my Lord and

Savior Jesus Christ for working His grace and power in me to surrender all of me to Him!

> *20 Now all glory to God, who is able, through his mighty power at work within us, to accomplish infinitely more than we might ask or think. 21 Glory to him in the church and in Christ Jesus through all generations forever and ever! Amen.*
> *Ephesians 3:20-21*

Dedication

I dedicate this book to my beautiful and wonderful wife of 32 years, Deborah. Apart from my salvation, you are the best blessing God has given me. Thank you for being my partner in ministry, my wife, and the mother of Alison, Jared, and Bret. You are my everything! I love you.

Foreword

In the terminology of the baseball world, Greg Mathis has hit a homerun! He not only stroked the ball out of the park—but he has done it with the bases loaded. In the constant and ever increasing flow of published Christian books, few will be as helpful and insightful to the family of faith as this one.

Greg has dared to address some issues many of us in the ministry have long known about but regretfully, have not wanted to talk about. In a sincere and candid manner he has shined the search light of God's Word squarely upon some delicate areas of our Christian walk that so often go unnoticed and unexamined. I am especially grateful that he has specifically addressed the matter of intemperance in eating habits and how the Lord has enabled him to effectively overcome it.

With his own unique and self-deprecating humor he has taken the reader on a frank and honest journey through his past failures as well as his present success. And thankfully, he has done that with Christian grace and kindness without undue censure and ridicule to those who have not yet been so fortunate as he.

I have carefully read this work and have given close attention to the author's spirit and manner. I rejoice that it is pure and without guile. It has little "Look what I have done" – but an abundance of "Look what God has done" reports. Although he is fortuitous enough to now be dwelling in a body that is slim and trim – he is wise enough to acknowledge that he still faces the battle of intemperance in his mind. He astutely understands that at the very best, the death of our flesh is only as long lasting as the depth of our commitment. A man who is wise enough not to forget where he once was has a much better chance of not going back. Greg has clearly reflected that truth in the wise and perceptive words of this book.

This most helpful volume needs to be read by every Christian. While not all Believers are overweight – every member of His Body needs to know what *it is like* to be overweight. For those who find themselves in the clutches of what seems a hopeless bondage to intemperance, these words will offer a fresh ray of hope, encouragement, and motivation. And for those who have never struggled with the problem of obesity, it will hopefully shine the light of kindness and compassion upon those who do.

Evangelist Junior Hill
Hartselle, Alabama

Table of Contents

Introduction

The journey of a thousand miles begins with one step.
> Chinese Proverb

Then Jesus said to his disciples, "If anyone would come after me, he must deny himself and take up his cross and follow me."
> Matthew 16:24

The strangest words come out of the mouths of children. I was sitting in my office one afternoon talking with a young family about Jesus, when one of their young girls asked me, "Why did Jesus have to die on the cross?" I told her, "Because of our sins." I then asked her if she knew what a sin was. She replied, "I think it's when we are doing something wrong in our life." I agreed, and carefully asked her if she felt she had ever done anything wrong. In other words, I was asking her if she considered herself a sinner. That's a big question for a seven year old to ponder. As she thought about it, she quickly pointed to her older sibling and said, "My sister is a big sinner!" Trying not to laugh, I softened the situation and explained that we are all sinners. I told her that:

- her <u>father</u> is a sinner
- her <u>mother</u> is a sinner
- her <u>sister</u> is a sinner (maybe even a big sinner)
- <u>she</u>, herself, is a sinner
- the Bible teaches <u>everyone</u> sins and does less than what God desires for us
- even <u>I</u> as a preacher am a sinner!

Her little eyes widened and she quickly asked, "Preacher, what kind of sins are you doing?" I told her that was personal and private, but I knew I was a sinner. I needed a Savior and found Him in Jesus. In a wonderful way, that young girl and her family received Jesus that day. However, the little girl's question about my sins kept echoing in my mind for weeks to come.

This book will tell of the journey I have taken in the previous year as I have tried to be honest about my sins and shortcomings. It has been an effort for me to be honest with God concerning areas in my life where He has convicted me. In many ways, I have even struggled to be honest with myself. What I am going to confess to you is not something I just recently learned about myself, but something I have known and struggled with for most of my life. I dare say a couple of things are going through your mind right now. "Preacher, what kind of sins have you been committing?" "And by the way, I also have shortcomings and sins that I struggle with in my life!"

In ministering to people for over three decades now, I know one thing for certain—each of us has something in our lives that hinders us from being everything we want to be, and more importantly, hinders us from being who God created us to be. I believe our struggles and hindrances are universal, but the obstacle is not always the same. Of course, as a minister of the Gospel, I believe we all have a sin problem that was solved and settled when Jesus died on the cross over two thousand years ago. As sinners, we need to turn to Him as our Savior in sincere repentance and faith. Let me ask you a few questions. Just how much of you do you believe Jesus wants to save? Your soul only? Or does Jesus want to save all of you—your body, soul, and spirit?

As Christians, we should remember we are only passing through this world and eternity should be our focus. Heaven is our home, and we are only left here on this earth for a little while. Truthfully, God usually leaves us here for a number of years after our salvation experience because He has a purpose for us while we reside here on this earth. I have also learned that spending time on earth before I go to Heaven is a real struggle. The Devil knows he can't get my soul (I gave that to Jesus at salvation), but he attacks my body, mind, and emotions every day. He tries to defeat me in my Christian walk. He wants me to embarrass Christ and even embarrass myself. I am sad to say that sometimes the Devil is more pleased with my actions than Jesus is. I can certainly relate to what the apostle Paul wrote in Romans concerning his own struggle with sin even after his conversion.

14 So the trouble is not with the law, for it is spiritual and good. The trouble is with me, for I am all too human, a slave to sin. 15 I don't really understand myself, for I want to do what is right, but I don't do it. Instead, I do what I hate. 16 But if I know that what I am doing is wrong, this shows that I agree that the law is good. 17 So I am not the one doing wrong; it is sin living in me that does it. 18 And I know that nothing good lives in me, that is, in my sinful nature.

*I want to do what is right, but I can't. 19 I want to do
what is good, but I don't. I don't want to do what is
wrong, but I do it anyway. 20 But if I do what I don't
want to do, I am not really the one doing wrong; it
is sin living in me that does it. 21 I have discovered
this principle of life—that when I want to do what is
right, I inevitably do what is wrong. 22 I love God's
law with all my heart. 23 But there is another power
within me that is at war with my mind. This power
makes me a slave to the sin that is still within me. 24
Oh, what a miserable person I am! Who will free me
from this life that is dominated by sin and death? 25
Thank God! The answer is in Jesus Christ our Lord.
So you see how it is: In my mind I really want to obey
God's law, but because of my sinful nature I am a
slave to sin.*
Romans 7:14-25

Why do I let the Devil occasionally get to me? Why do
I open the door for him? Why is it that some areas of my
life are reflective of the Lordship of Christ and other areas
appear to be controlled by the Devil, the world, or my own
weak flesh? Is God able to help me deal with these struggles?
Am I willing to allow God entry into every area of my life?
Simply put – *God is Able. But Am I Willing* to submit to His
ability to change me?

In this book, I will share what God is doing in my life. I am
certainly learning that He is more than able, but He has been
patiently waiting on me to be willing. I gave Him my soul as
a young boy. Since that time, my life has been a journey of
trying to surrender the rest of myself to Him on a daily basis.
It's as if the Lord has been saying to me, "You gave me your
soul, now give me the rest of you. Give me all that makes
you who you are—body, soul, and spirit." In this last year,
God has been pointedly working on my biggest obstacle to

His Lordship. I, along with many other Christians, have sung the words "I surrender all." This year, I have allowed those words to become a living spiritual reality. Now don't misunderstand, I certainly haven't arrived. I am simply saying that I am a little further down the road spiritually than where I was a year ago. It feels good! The will of God for our lives is that "good, perfect, and acceptable thing" according to the Apostle Paul. I don't want to turn back! I want to walk further with Him! Actually, I want to invite you to join me. God has impressed on my heart to write this book to remind myself of a few truths, and perhaps help you deal with some "strongholds" the Devil uses in our lives. These strongholds hold us back from being all God created and saved us to be. I am learning and enjoying that I can be "more than a conqueror" in Jesus. What a wonderful truth to realize that we can live a life of victory in Him!

My little four-year-old grandson asks me often to play a new game with him, and I sometimes find myself replying, "I don't know if I can do that." He then says to me, "Sure you can, Poppie!" As I have become honest with God about my life this year, I have seen that there are some areas which need to be addressed spiritually. I sometimes say, "God, can I really change my ways and conform to who and what You want me to be?" I have sensed God saying, "Sure you can!" He reminds me it's for this reason that:

- He created me
- He saved me
- He loves me
- He has a purpose for me
- He is the God of forgiveness and a second chance
- He (God) inspired the apostle Paul to write Romans 12:1-2

1 And so, dear brothers and sisters, I plead with you to give your bodies to God because of all he has done for you. Let them be a living and holy sacrifice—the kind he will find acceptable. This is truly the way to worship him. 2 Don't copy the behavior and customs of this world, but let God transform you into a new person by changing the way you think. Then you will learn to know God's will for you, which is good and pleasing and perfect.

Why don't you join me in making what time we have left here on earth a life of surrender? In his book, *The Pursuit of God*, A. W. Tozer said:

Father, I want to know Thee, but my coward heart fears to give up its toys. I cannot part with them without inward bleeding, and I do not try to hide from Thee the terror of the parting. I come trembling, but I do come. Please root from my heart all those things which I have cherished so long and which have become a very part of my living self, so that Thou mayest enter and dwell there without a rival. Then shalt Thou make the place of Thy feet glorious. Then shall my heart have no need of the sun to shine in it, for Thyself wilt be the light of it, and there shall be no night there. In Jesus' name, Amen.

Are you willing to take some steps in order to allow Jesus to dwell in your life without a rival? Are you ready to be honest with God about yourself? Honesty isn't easy, but it is the essential first step for you to become the person God created you to be!

Chapter 1

Step Toward Honesty

Honesty is the first chapter of the book of wisdom.
Thomas Jefferson

Kings take pleasure in honest lips.
Proverbs 16:13

The Greek philosopher, Plato, used to say, "An unexamined life is not worth living!" Lamentations 3:40 teaches, *Instead, let us test and examine our ways. Let us turn back to the LORD.* Being truly honest with oneself is not comfortable or easy. We are not eager to admit our weaknesses and shortcomings, especially to ourselves. It is at this point of admission, however, that real change can begin. The Bible teaches in Romans 3:23, *For everyone has sinned; we all fall short of God's glorious standard.* All of us have sins. We all are less than what God wants us to be. Charles Swindoll once said, "If sin were the color blue we would all be some shade of blue." In some areas of our life, we are very blue—I am talking "Papa Smurf" blue! On this journey, I first had to acknowledge the areas in my life which are unkempt and need attention. I have reflected long and hard on two piercing texts of Scripture.

First, Song of Solomon 1:6,

> *. . . My brothers were angry with me;*
> *they forced me to care for their vineyards,*
> *so I couldn't care for myself—<u>my own vineyard.</u>*

And second, Matthew 7:1-5,

> *"1 Do not judge others, and you will not be judged. 2 For you will be treated as you treat others. The standard you use in judging is the standard by which you will be judged. 3 "And why worry about a speck in your friend's eye when you have a log in your own? 4 How can you think of saying to your friend, 'Let me help you get rid of that speck in your eye,' when you can't see past the log in your own eye? 5 Hypocrite! <u>First get rid of the log in your own eye;</u> then you will see well enough to deal with the speck in your friend's eye."*

Many individuals may differ in their interpretation of these verses, but God personally convicted me that I, as a minister, was trying to help others with their vineyard while neglecting my <u>own</u>. I was trying to help others get the speck out of their eye while neglecting the log in my <u>own</u>. Ouch! Obviously, the challenge I faced was to examine my own life. Perhaps this is your challenge as well. As I began to examine my life, I was convicted of obvious areas that needed to be changed.

The truth is, at any given stage in our lives, sinful strongholds press against us. I guarantee many of you right now, if you will be honest, know exactly what weaknesses you face. This weakness may be a lack of discipline with your body, a lack of restraint over what goes into your mind, or possibly a failure to control your emotions. All of our sins and temptations fall into one of these categories. In the Bible, we see how the Devil attacked Eve's mind (Genesis 3:1-7), Job's body (Job 2), David's will (1 Chronicles 21), and Joshua's conscience (Zechariah 3). The Devil still attacks us in the same way. For example, if your predominant sin is a lack of control over your body, the sin may be adultery, fornication, homosexuality, gluttony, laziness, alcoholism, or drugs. If your struggle involves a battle in your mind, the sin may be identified as a problem with pride, pornography, lust, lying, envy, or jealousy. If mastering your emotions is a persistent internal conflict, then your situation may involve stress, depression, insecurity, frustration, guilt, bitterness, or a failure to forgive. The early church fathers felt great conviction about certain sins which haunt humanity. These sins were given the name of the "Seven Deadly Sins:"

- Lust
- Pride
- Greed
- Envy
- Anger
- Sloth (Laziness)
- Gluttony

John stated in 1 John 1:8-9 that we deceive ourselves if we claim to have no sin. What is your sin? Are you willing to be honest about it? What is it that dominates you the most? What sin plagues you on a consistent basis? If you had to take a piece of paper and make a list of your worst sins, which sin would be at the top? Understanding your sin is the first step to dealing with your stronghold, and is vitally important, so please don't put this book down now. You may be close to taking a step forward in the right direction. Pay attention — read and apply.

People are often blind to their problems. Unfortunately, the person with the problem is usually the last to realize or admit it. More than likely, you already know what your problem is, but you don't want to address or deal with it. Many individuals still try to convince themselves and others that they don't really have a problem. Is this you? Do you have a problem? Let me ask you a few questions:

- Is there a wrong that occurs consistently in your life on a daily, weekly, or monthly basis?
- Has this sin threatened your relationship and fellowship with God, family, and friends?
- Is this sin something that family, friends, or perhaps, a minister has attempted to confront in your life?
- Has God convicted you about this problem?
- Do you try to hide or cover up this sin, and would you be embarrassed if people really knew this about you?
- Have you ever made a New Year's resolution or a silent commitment in church to stop this sin?
- Would you be a better person if you dealt with this sin, and would your family and friends truly be proud of you?

I have found the answer to these questions to be revealing. It is very difficult to admit our failures and shortcomings. In the Bible, James says that a man may look in a mirror and not want to do anything about the person he sees.

*22 But don't just listen to God's word. You must do
what it says. Otherwise, you are only fooling yourselves. 23 For if you listen to the word and don't
obey, it is like glancing at your face in a mirror. 24
You see yourself, walk away, and forget what you
look like. 25 But if you look carefully into the perfect
law that sets you free, and if you do what it says and
don't forget what you heard, then God will bless you
for doing it.*
James 1:22-25

A step in the right direction starts with honesty and
confession. I had to start here, and your journey also begins
here. God loves us so much and wants to save us from the
Devil, the world, and ourselves. Because of that love, He
will convict us in areas where we are wrong and empower
us to change. Mark Twain said, "No one likes change but
a baby with a wet diaper." I can tell you that change feels
good if it brings your life—body, soul, and spirit—under the
Lordship of Christ.

When I began to think about my life and what God would
most like to change about me, I knew immediately that it
involved my eating habits and lack of exercise. Actually,
there are many things the Lord is addressing in me as He
molds me more into His likeness. But without a doubt, this
struggle was the one area of my life that clearly was not
under His Lordship. The Devil and the world attacked me
most often here, and for many years I had been more than a
willing participant. I use to say I weighed "two-hundred and
none of your business." For the last few years, I dropped the
two-hundred remark and just said, "None of your business."
One day I was on the scale sucking in air until my face was
red. My wife, Deborah, walked by and chuckled, "Sucking
in all that air won't make you weigh less!" I said back, "I am
not trying to weigh less but rather see the numbers!" Who

was I kidding? Anyone could look at me and tell I was more than just big-boned, more than physically mature. For a long time I even remarked that I wasn't overweight, just under-tall. If that were the case, I should have been 8'2"! I asked my wife one day if she had seen my belt around the house, and she responded, "Oh, will it go around the house now?" Let me quickly say that neither my family nor my church ever stopped loving me, but I didn't love myself and what I had become. Actually, there was becoming a lot of me not to love. Paul Lee Tan illustrates, "One asked Socrates why it was that Alcibiades, who was so brilliant and able a man, and had traveled so much, and seen so much of the world, was nevertheless so unhappy a man. Socrates replied, 'Because wherever he goes Alcibiades takes himself with him.'" That was me! Somehow I knew I wasn't who God wanted me to be. I felt somewhat ineffective preaching to others about their sins and shortcomings when I had some things I wasn't surrendering—when I wasn't being honest with myself.

I wonder if there might be something in your life that you aren't clearly surrendering? You can know your problem is a sin:

- If it violates God's Word.
- If you are being convicted of it by the Holy Spirit.
- If God has used your family or friends lovingly to encourage you to address this situation.
- If you won't, haven't, or can't seem to bring it under control!

So, day by day, week by week, month by month, and now year by year you continue giving in to this stronghold. The Devil only needs a "slightly open window" in our lives to beat us down and keep us from living the victorious Christian life. I don't know about you, but I was tired of failing. I confessed to God that with His help I was ready to do something about my stronghold. I am amazed at how much God loves me, forgives me, and readily helps me when I simply submit to Him. God is certainly able if we will only be available! Are you willing to let God help you in whatever area of your life He wants to change? I can promise this, moving toward the center of God's Will for your life will be the sweetest, most enjoyable time you will ever spend on earth. And, if you think you cannot overcome this problem (stronghold), just remember that "greater is He (God) that is within you than he (Devil) who is within the world."

If you are willing and ready, then step down this path with me. The chapters that follow are the steps I am taking in this journey. God is teaching me about true spiritual victory in my life—not just with my soul, but with all of me. This is a daily process of surrender to what God wants to do with all He created me to be. Obviously, we will never reach perfection until we get to Heaven, but our lives can be most fulfilling as we move toward spiritual maturity. The Devil tries to remind me of how ashamed I ought to be for not doing something sooner (sometimes he succeeds), but God reminds me that I am but "clay in the potter's hand." At least I am allowing Him access to areas that He has desired to mold for a long time! I am learning that when Jesus died on the cross, He did this not just to forgive my sins, but also to become Lord over my life. I must allow the cross not only to affect where I will spend eternity, but also to affect how I live my life.

In *The Man in the Mirror*, Patrick Morley told the following story. There was a pastor who wanted to get to know a church visitor who was a sports enthusiast. Since the pastor liked boxing, he invited the man to a boxing match, to which the man had never been. Just before the fight started, one of the boxers made the sign of the cross. "What does that mean?" asked the man. The pastor quickly replied, "It doesn't mean a thing if the guy can't box." Let me ask you, shouldn't the cross mean something in every area of your life? Jesus didn't die just to save your soul, but your whole being—mind, body, and spirit. Is every part of you living under the Lordship of Christ? In the following chapters, I am going to provide a step-by-step process that God is using to help me examine my sins and correct them. If you are willing to invest the time, you will discover all you can be in Christ and all He can be in you. Chris Lyans reminds us that Jesus "loves us just the way we are. And He loves us too much to let us stay the way we are." These words have become my thoughts and prayers over the last few months:

Thank you God for loving me so much that you gave Your Son, Jesus, to die on the cross for my sins. Also, thank you for promising to meet every need I have in mind, body, soul, and spirit. I am reminded in Romans 8:32, Since he did not spare even his own Son but gave him up for us all, won't he also give us everything else? Lord, teach me of the wonderful privileges I have as one of your children. Lord, teach me that I can change my ways and become the person you created me to be through Your Son, Jesus Christ.

God, who is wonderful, loving, and able to help you, is waiting. Are you willing to pray this same prayer? Are you willing to be honest admitting your stronghold? Are you willing to ask His help?

At the end of each chapter, I have included a section for your own personal reflection. You will find three focuses. First, in **"Steps Back,"** you will find a review of some of the crucial points of the chapter. Second, in **"Steps Into,"** you will find portions of Scripture highlighted in that chapter along with questions for introspection. Third, in **"Steps Forward,"** you will find application questions and suggestions for you to step closer to Christ in a growing relationship with Him.

Steps Back

√ "What is your sin? Are you willing to be honest about it? What is it that dominates you the most? What sin plagues you on a consistent basis?"

√ "Your problem is a sin: If it violates God's Word; If you are being convicted of it by the Holy Spirit; If God has used your family or friends lovingly to encourage you to address this situation; If you won't, haven't, or can't seem to bring it under control!"

Steps Into

√ Song of Solomon 1:6 emphasizes, *...so I couldn't care for myself—my own vineyard.*

Does that describe you? Have you failed to care for yourself as God would intend?

√ Matthew 7:5 teaches to *First get rid of the log in your own eye; then you will see well enough to deal with the speck in your friend's eye.*

Are you addressing your own "log"?

Steps Forward

√ The first step in the journey to freedom is confession. Have you admitted to yourself and confessed to God your stronghold? If you have not done so, feel free to use the margin below to confess to God your stronghold. If you feel uncomfortable writing it out, take a moment and pray, confessing it to God.

√ In a later chapter, I will deal with the importance of accountability, but you may even now want to find a friend, relative, or pastor to whom you can confess your stronghold.

Chapter 2

Step Toward Evaluation

I know of no more encouraging fact than the unquestioning ability of man to evaluate his life by a conscious endeavor.
Henry David Thoreau

Don't think you are better than you really are. Be honest in your evaluation of yourselves, measuring yourselves by the faith God has given us.
Romans 12:3

B ecause we often equate our souls with our spiritual side, we miss the connection between the discipline of our bodies and our spiritual service to the Lord. For many years, I served the Lord with a body that was unhealthy as a result of poor eating habits and a lack of exercise. God has recently changed the way I think about my body through a passage of scripture found in 1 Corinthians 9:24–27.

24 Don't you realize that in a race everyone runs, but only one person gets the prize? So run to win! 25 All athletes are disciplined in their training. They do it to win a prize that will fade away, but we do it for an eternal prize. 26 So I run with purpose in every step. I am not just shadowboxing. 27 I discipline my <u>body</u> like an athlete, training it to do what it should. Otherwise, I fear that after preaching to others I myself might be <u>disqualified</u>.

I was familiar with this passage, but I never really made the connection between a disciplined physical body and being qualified for spiritual service. What exactly is Paul teaching here? He is speaking about the fact that we will one day stand in judgment as Christians for how well we disciplined our bodies. Paul writes that just as an athlete would strive to be physically fit for a competition through strict physical discipline, we, as Christians, need to apply this kind of discipline to stay spiritually and physically healthy for ministry. If you have ever been around an individual who trained for an athletic event and took it seriously, his or her level of commitment is phenomenal. An athlete in training will sacrifice, deprive themselves, and say "no" to anything and everyone that might threaten their goal. Paul writes that Christians must have a much higher goal in life, and we should strive to "stay the course, fight a good fight, and finish the race." No one can do this effectively—physically or spiritually—without discipline. Interestingly, Paul coupled these two truths together. We should:

- Practice physical discipline
- Avoid spiritual disqualification

I began to ponder how we might spiritually disqualify ourselves because of a lack of physical discipline. I had never really thought about this very much. I have known some ministers and other church leaders who couldn't control physical passions concerning sexual desires. Unfortunately, they became sexually involved outside the bounds of marriage and lost their level of ministry effectiveness. Sadly, they cut short their ministry potential. Surely, to some degree, this is what Paul is talking about. I have also known Christians and ministers who rendered themselves ineffective because they couldn't control their emotions. Anger and depression have robbed many talented saints of opportunities to serve God in an effective way. When you add an inability to forgive and bitterness to these emotions, the situation can be overwhelming to both the person experiencing these feelings and those who are the recipient of these emotions. We have all heard the statement, "They would surely be effective as Christians if they could just control their emotions." Anger robbed Moses from going into the Promised Land!

But, I have also come to realize that there may be something else very significant that can rob us of effectively serving the Lord. If someone does not practice proper habits with eating and exercise, he may not have the right amount of energy to minister at his highest level of effectiveness. This person could even damage their body so much that they die at a younger age and cut short what could have been a longer, more effective ministry on earth. Do you believe this? God convicted me that I had the potential to be one such person. Sadly, I have lost dear friends through the years, perhaps for this very reason. Can a person die prematurely? I think they can, and they have! This premature death may be the fault of others, but it may also be brought about by the personal actions of the individual. I don't think a Christian can live a day longer than God wills for their lives, but I do think we, as Christians, in disobedience to God's Word, can prematurely cut our lives short. If a Christian commits suicide or drives recklessly causing a fatal car accident, was that God's will for their lives? Of course not! Neither is it God's will for us to eat ourselves into an early grave!

My friend, Sam Varner, once asked me, "How long do you want to live and why?" I told him I wanted to live until I was 75 years of age to preach the gospel and also to be here for my family. He then gently asked, "If you don't change your eating habits and your lack of exercise, do you really think that will happen?" I sadly said, "No, it will probably not happen." I want you to know that I realize some very fit, slim people can and do die at a younger age, and that some very unhealthy, obese people live to an old age. However, this fact gave me little solace as God convicted me of my unhealthy lifestyle concerning food and exercise. Although I knew this was important, what really challenged me was the realization that one day I was going to give an account for the disciplining (or lack thereof) of my body at the Judgment Seat of Christ. I am convinced this is so relevant to us because I believe every sin we commit is in the body.

- It may be a sin in the mind.
- It might be a sin with the emotions and will.
- It could be a sin in the flesh.

Take every sin that you are aware of, or take your own sinful stronghold now, and see how it is connected to your body.

- Lust with the <u>eyes</u>
- Gossip with the <u>ears</u> and <u>mouth</u>
- Profanity and drunkenness with the <u>mouth</u>
- Stealing with the <u>hands</u>
- Adultery, fornication, and homosexuality with the <u>body</u>
- Covetousness with the <u>eyes</u>
- Gluttony with the <u>mouth</u>

Did Jesus not teach us that many of these things need to be confronted in the heart and mind before they ever manifest themselves in the flesh? I don't want to arrive in Heaven one day to see what I might have done for the Lord if I had been more disciplined with my body. At the judgment, would God possibly show me a healthy, fit Greg Mathis ministering for Him? How could I possibly love food and laziness more than I love Jesus? I was sinning in this undisciplined area of my life by not having my body under the Lordship of Christ. Bill Hybels said,

Isn't it time we got serious about what we do with our bodies as Christians including what we eat and how we exercise? Our goal isn't vain or temporal. Our goal is to be available for eternal purposes for the longest amount of time, with the greatest amount of energy, and the highest degree of emotional, mental, and spiritual well being. We owe it to God to be faithful stewards of the bodies He has given us.

My family, friends, and my doctor would often try to talk to me about this stronghold of unhealthy eating and lack of exercise. I would say I didn't want to talk about it, or I would make some kind of humorous remark. God finally got my attention, saying that He wanted to talk to me about this matter now! As I move closer to the Judgment Seat of Christ, God does not desire that I come with such an unhealthy stronghold in my life. In this particular area, how could I be so indifferent toward self-denial, daily discipline, and physical and spiritual stamina? Just as it takes a disciplined athlete to stay on course, a Christian must be disciplined to stay on the spiritual course God has laid out for him in the world. If athletes will discipline their bodies for the opportunity to wear wreaths, hang gold medals around their necks, hold plaques, or hoist trophies in the air, how much more should we, as Christians, discipline our bodies to one day hear Jesus say, "Well done thy good and faithful servant?" Believe me, in particular areas of my life, our Savior would not compliment me this way. Actually, I am convinced in the areas of eating and exercise, Jesus would have told me how I set a bad example and was a poor steward of the body He had given me. Perhaps you feel the same way. As a child of God, how can we not be focused and faithful in every area of life, including our areas of struggle? We will never accomplish this without self-control and discipline. Remember that the Devil wants us to stumble. Because of this, he will attack any vulnerable area of our bodies. For me, this vulnerable area was how much I ate and how little I exercised. For you, this area may be something else. In any way he can, the Devil wants to defeat us.

The Bible is full of examples of successes and failures. Some saints stayed faithful to God and are listed as successful examples for us to follow. Others failed. Do you know what I have observed as the difference between those who were faithful and those who failed? Discipline! Those saints who succeeded exercised discipline and those who showed little or no discipline did not. This is still true today. There is certainly nothing easy about staying on course spiritually. It requires daily discipline. When someone asks us to refrain from overeating, they are saying, "Exercise some discipline." When you hear someone ask you to put a program on your computer that will protect against pornography, that's discipline. When a preacher encourages you not to become a listening ear to gossip, this takes discipline. When a parent pleads with their teenager to stay pure sexually and wait until marriage for sexual relations, they are asking for discipline. The Bible exhorts us to discipline in Proverbs 25:28. *A person without self-control is like a city with broken-down walls.* Jerry Bridges said, "Self-control is the believer's wall of defense against the sinful desires that wage war against my soul." A Christian without self-control in even one area of his life becomes easy prey for the Devil. He will attack this vulnerable area, leaving a Christian to be less than who God saved him to be. Common sense tells us to avoid excesses and learn to regulate our appetites. We all have a tendency to overindulge in areas of our lives: food, sex, alcohol, gossip, anger, and other habits. This overindulgence usually develops into enormous appetites for something or someone. We all experience difficulties in saying "yes" or "no" to certain things, people, or places. In the Bible, James writes in 1:14 that it is these desires within us that set us up for failure. *Temptation comes from our own desires, which entice us and drag us away.* Jesus was talking about discipline and self-control when He spoke the following words in Luke 9:23: *Then he said to the crowd, "If any of you wants to be my follower, you must turn from your selfish ways, take up your cross daily, and follow me."*

If we are going to follow Jesus faithfully, we must learn to control our inner passions and desires. We must present the Lord our bodies as a daily discipline to protect ourselves from becoming slaves to anything else. Paul reminds us in 1 Corinthians 6:12, *You say, "I am allowed to do anything"—but not everything is good for you. And even though "I am allowed to do anything," I must not become a slave to anything.* I literally had become a slave to food and laziness. I wasn't lazy in sermon preparation, pastoral duties, or providing for my family. Many would say I am a disciplined, hard worker in these areas. However, in the areas of how much I ate and how little I exercised, I was an obvious undisciplined failure. In one instance, a lady tried to squeeze into the elevator with me, and asked me to "move my beer gut." I responded to her that I was a Baptist preacher and didn't have a beer gut. She quickly corrected her assertion, and replied, "Well, move that chicken coop out of the way." Certainly, I had eaten a lot of chicken right into the ministry, and it showed. My belt looked like a leather fence around a chicken graveyard. It hurts me to confess that to you, but honest evaluation is a part of genuine confession and repentance. My stronghold was obvious, while yours might be more secretive. Even so, confession and repentance are required to come under the Lordship of Jesus Christ. My new lifestyle verse while I remain here on earth is 1 Corinthians 10:31. *So whether you eat or drink, or whatever you do, do it all for the glory of God.* This verse speaks directly to the area of my stronghold. It forces me to intentionally evaluate my actions including my eating habits and exercise schedule.

Now, lest you think I never have a weak moment, let me confess something to you. I never can drive by Doris Waldrop's house without thinking about her biscuits. They are so good they will make your tongue beat your brains right out of your head. I often have to pray this prayer:

Lord,
Forgive me for even thinking about Doris Waldrop's
tomato biscuits with mayo, heavy on both sides, and
with some of her banana pudding for dessert.
Amen.

I feel better now! Seriously, for several months I have been practicing discipline in what I eat and daily exercise. I have applied 1 Timothy 4:7 to this process. *Do not waste time arguing over godless ideas and old wives' tales. Instead, train yourself to be godly.*

Instead of living to eat, I am currently learning how I can eat to live, preach, and be around for my family. God may take me home tomorrow, but at least I am living each day with a spiritually healthy mindset. I am seeking to correct my shortcomings and learning to allow God to shape me spiritually by leading me to discipline my body physically. As a result, I feel better about myself physically and spiritually than I have for years. I cannot help but thank God daily for giving me the opportunity to address this sinful stronghold before He calls me home. Has this sin been a struggle in my life? Yes! By the way, you may be wondering why I would address a sin related to food. I say why not write about it. Do you realize that the first sin was related to food? Adam and Eve ate "forbidden fruit" from the one tree that God instructed them to leave alone. My tree was full of "forbidden food" that was killing me slowly—fried chicken, peanut butter, mayonnaise, oatmeal cakes, made-from-scratch biscuits, banana pudding, and so many others! But thank God that He is giving me the opportunity to change. Would you like to do the same? Ephesians 4:22-24 means more to me today than ever before. *22 Throw off your old sinful nature and your former way of life, which is corrupted by lust and deception. 23 Instead, let the Spirit renew your thoughts and attitudes. 24 Put on your new nature, created to be like God—truly righteous and holy.*

Jonathan Edwards lived out his life with this motto, "I won't do anything I wouldn't be willing to do if it were the last hour of my life. I refuse to ever give in or over to my weaknesses, nor ever stop fighting against them." I want to be like that, and I want to encourage you to join me. We may have different strongholds looming over us like a big question mark, but the answer for all of us is God. God is bigger than any stronghold! As I have surrendered to Him, He is faithfully helping me overcome those things that would threaten me.

This is a slow process. As I evaluated my life, I didn't become overweight and undisciplined overnight, and I won't change all I need to change overnight. This is also a daily process of diligently and constantly exercising discipline. Shouldn't this really be the Christian life for all of us? The Christian life is a daily surrender to the only One who can help us: the Lord Jesus Christ. Seneca said, "All my life I have been seeking to climb out of the pit of my besetting sins, and I cannot do it and I never will unless a hand is let down to draw me up." In Matthew 11:28-30, Jesus is extending to all of us a hand saying, *"Come to me, all of you who are weary and carry heavy burdens, and I will give you rest. 29 Take my yoke upon you. Let me teach you, because I am humble and gentle at heart, and you will find rest for your souls. 30 For my yoke is easy to bear and the burden I give you is light."*

As I did with my soul, I now say to the Lord with my body, "Precious Lord, take my hand. Lead me on, let me stand..." He is more than able to do the same for you, if you are willing. To remain undisciplined in any area of our lives only makes us a headache to ourselves, a heartache to others, and a threat to become disqualified for spiritual service. I would hate to think that I would allow anyone or anything to keep me from being all God created me to be. I was saved by grace, and I serve Him by grace. I realize that I was saved to do good things for our Lord. One of these things is to care for the body (temple) I was given while I live on earth. God never saved me to live for the Devil, the world, or my own flesh. Understanding this truth has taken a while—too long, in fact—but it has begun to sink in. This is biblical evaluation, and it leads to repentance and correction. Will you evaluate yourself? Will you step forward from there to allow the Lord to convict you? Please continue to read, and I will tell you how this happened in my life.

Steps Back

√   "I believe this is so relevant to us because I believe every sin we commit is in the body. It may be a sin in the mind. It might be a sin with the emotions and will. It could be a sin in the flesh."

√ "If we are going to follow Jesus faithfully, we must learn to control our inner passions and desires. We must present the Lord our bodies as a daily discipline to protect ourselves from becoming slaves to anything else."

Steps Into

√ Romans 12:3 teaches, *Don't think you are better than you really are. Be honest in your evaluation of yourselves, measuring yourselves by the faith God has given us.*

Do you understand the importance of honestly evaluating yourself? How often would you say you evaluate your spiritual walk? Family relationships? Work ethic? Eating habits? Exercise habits? Do any of these areas need a thorough evaluation?

√ 1 Corinthians 10:31 states, *So whether you eat or drink, or whatever you do, do it all for the glory of God.*

Everything you do—including eating and exercise— should bring glory to God. Do your daily habits and lifestyle bring glory to God? Would you say that your eating and exercise habits bring glory to God?

Steps Forward

√ Set aside a time to thoroughly evaluate one significant area of your life. Be honest with yourself and God. Identify exactly where you stand in that area. Set a goal (or goals) to evaluate your life more regularly and thoroughly.

√ Take an average day. Would God be glorified by none of it, some of it, or most of it?

Chapter 3

Step Toward Identity

The most common form of despair is not being who you are.
Soren Kierkegaard

This means that anyone who belongs to Christ has become a new person. The old life is gone; a new life has begun!
2 Corinthians 5:17

As we address problems in our Christian lives, I believe that we often miss a crucially important truth: who we are in Jesus Christ. I think we are fairly clear on who we will be in Heaven (perfect), but we sometimes struggle with who we can be in Christ now (conquerors). If someone were to ask you who you are in Christ, how would you respond? Learning who Christ is in us and who we are in Him is essential in every area of our life. This is especially critical when dealing with our strongholds. We must understand that when Jesus died on the cross for our sins, He not only paid the penalty for our sins, He also delivered us from the power of sin. This means that Jesus has made it possible for us to choose to do the right thing on a daily basis.

Now, a few responsibilities in the Christian life seem to come easy for me. Many of the commandments Jesus asks me to obey are a joy and pleasure. In some areas of my life I rarely struggle. On the other hand, areas such as diet and exercise are like a plague to me. I often feel like what Hosea described as a "half-baked cake" (Hosea 7:1-10). It shouldn't surprise you that I would be thinking of a cake! Actually, I'm thinking about Betsy Bailey's 7-layer chocolate cake. Delicious! Some cakes may be unacceptable when they come out of the oven to the one who has worked so hard to bake them. Have you ever eaten a slice of a half-baked cake?

Years ago, when we lived in the church parsonage, we had an old oven that wouldn't heat evenly. Sometimes, Deborah would bake one of her famous pound cakes and find that it was cooked on one side and gooey on the other. She considered it inedible. So did I—after five slices! You might be wondering, "Was that gooey part good?" Listen, the worst piece of pound cake I've ever had was fantastic! On a more serious note, Hosea used this half-baked cake to illustrate the lack of consistency in the lives of people. It certainly reminds me of my own life. There are areas in my life where I do satisfactorily, but other areas I have not addressed and developed. When Jesus died on the cross, did His shed blood *fully* cover all my weaknesses and shortcomings? Did He *completely* deliver me from the power of sin? Does God *actually* give me the Holy Spirit to empower me to have victory in everything, including my biggest struggle? Is this what Paul meant in Romans 6:14 when he wrote, *Sin is no longer your master, for you no longer live under the requirements of the law. Instead, you live under the freedom of God's grace.*

If this is true, why do I persistently seem to be shackled to struggles in some areas of my life? Why am I able to win some battles handily but constantly lose others? Can I truly get out from under the mastery of this sin that causes me such misery? I know this is what God desires me to do, and deep inside it is really what I want to do—but how? How do I separate myself from this problem?

God's Word teaches us that we should stay clear from anything or anyone that would control us. That's what Paul was addressing in 1Thessalonians 4:3-5: *3 God's will is for you to be holy, so stay away from all sexual sin. 4 Then each of you will control his own body and live in holiness and honor—5 not in lustful passion like the pagans who do not know God and his ways.* Obviously, the struggle in this scripture concerns a sexual sin, but wouldn't this verse apply to any struggle? I also think about Paul's teaching in Ephesians 1:4: *Even before he made the world, God loved us and chose us in Christ to be holy and without fault in his eyes.* Paul implicitly taught that if I allow this struggle to linger in my life, this would be contrary to the very purpose for which God saved me. God wants me to address my struggles and live obediently. Notice Titus 2:11-12: *11 For the grace of God has been revealed, bringing salvation to all people. 12 And we are instructed to turn from godless living and sinful pleasures. We should live in this evil world with wisdom, righteousness, and devotion to God.*

Surely, I must bring any struggle under His control! Now, lest I be misunderstood, I am not talking about living a perfect, sinless life. That is impossible. I do believe as we grow close to Jesus and become more like Him, His Lordship and our spiritual growth should be more obvious in our lives. 2 Timothy 2:21 states, *If you keep yourself pure, you will be a special utensil for honorable use. Your life will be clean, and you will be ready for the Master to use you for every good work.* Perhaps you agree with me so far, but you are still asking, "How?" I think many of us have the desire to improve and live more like Christ, but we don't know <u>how</u>. Why can't we obtain victory in certain areas of our lives? Why don't we experience the truth of Romans 6:6-7? *6 We know that our old sinful selves were crucified with Christ so that sin might lose its power in our lives. We are no longer slaves to sin. 7 For when we died with Christ we were set free from the power of sin.*

We know that the Bible teaches victory, but we simply don't experience spiritual success in particular areas of our lives. <u>Why?</u> What does it take to experience what many have called the "victorious Christian life?" I remember the first time I heard that phrase. I was in seminary and heard that a Christian can experience victorious living. Colossians 1:27 explains, *For God wanted them to know that the riches and glory of Christ are for you Gentiles, too. And this is the secret: <u>Christ lives in you.</u> This gives you assurance of sharing his glory.*

When I began to grasp this concept, I was so eager to learn and experience all that Christ wanted to do in me! I often felt like the description given in the poem by Mrs. Charles E. Cowman titled "Wits End,"

Are you standing at "Wits End Corner"
Christian, with troubled brow?
Are you thinking of what is before
You and all you are bearing now?
Does all the world seem against you
And you are in the battle alone?
Remember...at "Wits End Corner"
Is just where God's power is shown!

I prayed, "Lord, show me your power!" I know I began to experience inner renewal and spiritual growth. Since this event, God has prospered my life and ministry in profound spiritual ways. Even so, certain areas of my life were not under His Lordship. If Jesus is my Savior and Lord, why do I struggle to turn particular areas of my life over to Him? Why have you not also conquered your weaknesses?

It is easy to play the "blame game" at this point. We are living in a society where people blame everyone but themselves for their own failures and shortcomings. It's my family, my work, my circumstances, my environment—anything but me. I blamed my eating habits and lack of exercise on my family background. The Osborne side of my family is notorious for the way they eat, but my whole family tree is fairly good at it. I blamed my schedule, the stress of the ministry, and those always wanting to feed me as a minister. I gladly told the story about the time Mrs. Kate Miller baked me another one of her famous "black bottom pies" (melted chocolate on bottom and custard on the top). When she gave it to me, I told her I was just getting bigger and bigger. She responded, "Don't worry preacher, no one should ever trust a skinny preacher!" Well, if that was the case, I was becoming the most trustworthy preacher in the country! I finally had to come to the place where I admitted, "You know what my problem is—it's me!"

I was my own worst enemy. No one was at fault but me. Honestly, in the area of eating and lack of exercise, I was doing what my flesh wanted. I was unhealthy because my flesh desired to be unhealthy, and I didn't exercise properly because I was too lazy. Ouch! Jesus wasn't failing me, I was causing my own failure. I was still clearly in control in some areas of my life, and my weight was one such area. Who was I deceiving but myself? Surely, I wasn't going to blame all the extra weight on the Lord, was I? I know my body is His "temple," but for crying out loud, *was I building a synagogue?*

I had become an embarrassment not only to myself, but to the Lord. After several months of healthy eating, exercise, and considerable weight loss, one person said to me when I was at the gym, "What a testimony!" Well, what was I before, a bad testimony? Yes, in that area of my life I was! No matter how loudly I preached, I exhibited a noticeable failure with my weight, which proved that I was not practicing everything I preached!

You and I must realize that God does not force His will on us. Like Adam and Eve, we have a choice. I can choose Jesus or reject Him. Even if I choose Jesus in salvation, I may still betray His Lordship in the daily struggle to give Him control of my life. While Jesus has owned my soul since I was eight years of age, I only recently have become serious about giving Him my body. This problem isn't unique to me; it's the struggle of every born-again Christian. It is our problem with ourselves. I want you to read a portion from Jack Taylor's book, *The Key to Triumphant Living,* as he accurately portrays where many of us currently are in the struggles within ourselves:

> *"When man did what Satan wanted him to do, he became infected with the same disease of SELF. He then possessed a nature incorrigible to God. Self became the archenemy. Another word for self is the "flesh." This is what we are without Christ. "They that are in the flesh [self] cannot please God" (Rom. 8:8).*
>
> *Self is not subject to the law of God, nor can it ever be. "Because the carnal mind is enmity against God: For it is not subject to the law of God neither indeed can be" (Rom. 8:7). Self cannot be <u>domesticated</u>. This is a vital point which kept me from victory*

for many years. I thought surely that something must have happened to my "self" nature when I got saved. Years after my conversion I heard a preacher say that nothing happened to that self when I got saved, absolutely nothing. It didn't improve one iota! Now, isn't that shocking? Christ didn't come in to improve self but to replace it. Self has no place in the economy of God.

Neither can you discipline it. How busy we are trying to discipline self. But it is hopelessly incorrigible. It is wild and deceitful. You can educate it, change its living conditions, and expose it to the highest kind of morality, but self is still "deceitful above all things and desperately wicked." There is no "good" self and "bad" self as far as God is concerned. The self-life represents everything foreign to the nature of God. Wherever its nature is manifest, there is "adultery, fornication, uncleanness, lasciviousness, idolatry, witchcraft, hatred, variance, emulations, wrath, strife, seditions, heresies, envyings, murders, drunkenness, revelings, and such like" (Gal. 5:19-21)

Certainly "self," which is you and me, gets in the way. Why would I blame others when I have no one to blame but myself? The truth is, I've had more trouble with myself than any person I have ever encountered. I am the most difficult person I have ever had to manage. I keep getting in the way of what God wants to do in my life. The Devil is more than glad to assist me in my displays of selfishness. I will never manage or discipline self; I must die to self daily. Self, left alone, will gladly become a cooperating partner with Satan to do something destructive.

In an old book by Hannah Whitall Smith, *The Christian's Secret of a Happy Life,* a classic on living the victorious life, she reminds us of how the Devil will oppose our every step of spiritual progress. "The Devil will do everything he can, on a daily basis, to keep us from giving every area of our lives to the Lord. The Devil especially likes to hold onto a stronghold or two in our lives. Anything to keep us from becoming all God saved us to become." Surely, as Christians, this is not what we want for ourselves, and I know this is not what God desires. Still, a question looms heavily, "How can I ever change this?"

Obviously, I cannot simply decide to change myself with enough willpower. I can read the *Nike* slogan "Just Do It" all I want, but in particular areas of my life it simply doesn't work. We all likely have strongholds in our lives to prove this fact. I only have to look at pictures of myself over the course of the last twenty years to obviously understand that the only time I "just did it" was when I ate the whole bag of hot dogs from Hot Dog World! Clearly, any energy of the flesh I could muster up took me in the wrong direction (usually back to the buffet).

Pay careful attention as I explain what God has taught me spiritually. I realized that this issue was not a matter of what I could do, but what Jesus could do in me. I had to learn that what happened to me in salvation (where Jesus did it all) also happens in sanctification (where only Jesus can daily mold me into what He wants me to be). To begin experiencing victory over my strongholds, I must daily die to self and allow Jesus to live His life in me. In other words, I must let Jesus make decisions for me in every aspect of my life. I ought to ask Jesus each day, "Jesus, do You want me to eat healthy today, with moderation?" or "Do you want me to overeat like a glutton?" "Jesus, would You like me to spend an hour exercising this body You have given me?" or "Would you be more pleased with me sitting a little longer in my Lazy Boy recliner eating another peanut butter, banana, and mayonnaise sandwich?" It is very sobering to ask Jesus if I have His permission to neglect myself today. When given the opportunity, the Lord can be clear with His answers to these questions. You may ask if He answers audibly, but I believe He answers us much louder than if he answered audibly. For the last several months, He has told me every day to eat healthy and exercise regularly. He has also reminded me that when He was here on earth, He didn't become healthy, strong and fit by having poor eating habits and laziness! Remember, Jesus walked everywhere He traveled. He chose daily to live a healthy lifestyle, both physically and spiritually, and if I will allow Him, He will lead me to live in the same manner.

I had to decide who would control my choices and situations daily. I came to grips with Romans 6:12, *Do not let sin control the way you live; do not give in to sinful desires.* The phrase, "Do not let sin" pierced me because my lack of discipline was controlling me. I was responsible! Even now, I must choose who or what will reign over my life. I have an old nature (self) and a new nature (Christ), and each day, hundreds of decisions reveal which of these natures rules me.

An additional truth from this verse, drawn from the context of Romans 6, states that I don't have to give in to self. In light of Jesus' work on the cross, we do not have to be ruled by sin's power. Because He is now in me, and I am now in Him, I am not ruled by sin anymore. People who do not know Jesus can't help but submit to sin, but Christians have a choice, in the power of Christ, to renounce sin's reign over them. I had to be willing to make this choice concerning the stronghold of unhealthy eating and lack of exercise. You must make this choice with your stronghold!

We must know that in salvation, Christ not only made a way for our souls to escape from hell, He also made a way for us to escape our strongholds! Wow! I think I have known this truth, and even preached it, but I have only truly experienced it recently. What freedom you will experience when you apply this truth to the struggle you are enduring with your stronghold. Lay hold to this wonderful truth and live out Romans 6:11, *So you also should consider yourselves to be dead to the power of sin and alive to God through Christ Jesus.* Jesus has already won the victory for us, if we will simply say "no" to ourselves and "yes" to Him. In Jesus, we can live the victorious Christian life!

I want to teach you something that has greatly helped me in dealing with my stronghold. The next time you are faced with a decision, I encourage you to try this exercise. Hold up your right hand, which represents God's word, way, and will for your life. Your right hand stands for the right thing to do. Then, hold up your left hand which represents your flesh, the world, and the Devil. Remind yourself that if you choose to give in to sin and self, you leave the will and way of God. I have actually gone as far as holding up that banana sandwich (yes, with peanut butter and mayonnaise) in my left hand and then holding up the Bible in my right hand, asking which will control me. I currently practice this exercise in my mind with every decision I face. You see, Jesus deserves to control every decision I make because He loves me, He died for me, and He wants to mold me into His image. Not only did He deliver me from the penalty and power of sin, He continues to deliver me every day. I simply need to start living for Jesus—my Savior and Lord—and not the desires of my flesh or the appetites of my body.

As you will see in the next chapter, daily dying to self is a lifelong process! I cannot improve upon the words of Jerry Bridges in his book, *The Pursuit of Holiness,*

> *"It is our habit to live for ourselves and not for God. When we become Christians, we do not drop all this overnight. In fact, we will spend the rest of our*

lives putting off these habits and putting on habits of holiness.

Not only have we been slaves to sin, but we still live in a world populated by slaves of sin. The conventional values around us reflect this slavery, the world tries to conform us to its own sinful mold.

Therefore, though sin no longer reigns in us, it will constantly try to get at us. Though we have been delivered from the kingdom of sin and its rule, we have not been delivered from its attacks." As Dr. Martin Lloyd-Jones says in his exposition of Romans 6, "though sin cannot reign in us, that is, in our essential personality, it can, if left unchecked, reign in our mortal bodies. It will turn the natural instincts of our bodies into lust. It will turn our natural appetites in indulgence, our need for clothing and shelter into materialism, and our normal sexual interest into immorality." You and I are living examples of this truth!

That is why Paul exhorted us to be on our guard so that we will not let sin reign in our bodies. Before our salvation, before our death to the reign of sin, such an exhortation would have been futile. You cannot say to a slave, "Live as a free man," if he still is enslaved to something or someone. If we are free in Jesus then with His help nothing should control me but Him! We are to keep before us this fact that we are no longer slaves to sin, self, Satan, or the world. We can now stand up to sin and say no to it. Before we had no choice; now we have one. When we sin as Christians, we do not sin as slaves, but as individuals with the freedom of choice. We sin because we choose to sin.

You and I must fully understand this truth and admit it. Something is desperately wrong with us spiritually if we continue to give in to the same sinful strongholds in our lives. For a Christian, this lifestyle is unacceptable! I had to come to the place where I stopped saying, "Jesus, You can control everything but my eating habits and lack of exercise." I had to come to the place where I said, "Jesus, I surrender all! Here is Greg Mathis, all of me, nothing withheld." D.L. Moody surmised, "This present age has not yet seen what God will do with one man or woman, boy or girl, who will turn everything over to Him." That includes all of the strongholds in our lives. I keep the words of the poem "Take Over" by Ruth Harms Calkin on my desk as a reminder of what I need to say and do in surrendering everything to our Lord.

> At first, Lord, I asked You
> To take sides with me.
> With David the Psalmist
> I circled and underlined:
> "The Lord if for me..."
> "Maintain my rights, O Lord..."
> "Let me stand above my foes..."
> But with all my pleading
> I lay drenched in darkness
> Until in utter confusion I cried
> "Don't take sides, Lord,
> Just take over."
> And suddenly it was morning.

If you and I are truly interested in change, we must first be willing to surrender everything. Are you interested in coming to the place where you will allow the Lord to completely take over your life without hesitation and with total surrender? If you are, continue reading and get ready for a radical lifestyle change concerning the strongholds in your life that have been holding you back.

Steps Back

√ "Pay careful attention as I explain what God has taught me spiritually...I had to learn that what happened to me in salvation (where Jesus did it all) also happens in sanctification (where only Jesus can daily mold me into what He wants me to be). To begin experiencing victory over my strongholds, I must daily die to self and allow Jesus to live His life in me. In other words, I must let Jesus make decisions for me in every aspect of my life."

√ "I had to come to the place where I stopped saying, 'Jesus, You can control everything but my eating habits and lack of exercise.' I had to come to the place where I said, 'Jesus, I surrender all! Here is Greg Mathis, all of me, nothing withheld.'"

Steps Into

√ Romans 6:14 teaches, *Sin is no longer your master... Instead, you live under the freedom of God's grace.*

Because I live in the freedom of God's grace, I no longer have to be subject to the power of sin. Does that verse describe the condition of my life?

- Colossians 1:27 explains, *And this is the secret: Christ lives in you.*

- Do I realize that Christ AND His power to overcome sin reside in me?

Steps Forward

- Who is in charge of my life—me or Christ? Explain your answer.

- Jesus wants to replace my selfishness with His identity—with His power and grace. He wants my life to look like Him. How would my life be different if I looked more like Jesus and less like me? Family? Job? Leisure time?

Chapter 4

Step Toward His Lordship

I gave in, and admitted that God was God.
    C. S. Lewis

Christ died and rose again for this very purpose—to be Lord both of the living and of the dead.
    Romans 14:9

Allowing the Lord to completely take over your life is not easy. I readily give Him some things in my life. I gladly gave Him my soul when I was eight years old. I didn't need to hear many old-fashioned sermons about Hell before I understood that I didn't want to be there for one day, much less eternity. I gladly give the Lord my problems, which are always too heavy for me to carry. Although worry has never really been an issue for me, I do realize that for some reading this book, worry and fretting will be the Devil's stronghold in your life. As I reflect on my life, I see how I have given

Jesus most of myself with ease, but I have had great difficulty in surrendering my entire life to His Lordship. Unfortunately, I desire to retain control of a few things, or a few things desire to control me. Our struggles may be different, but our spiritual solution is the same. Each one of us has a stronghold in our lives. This book will help you understand and address your stronghold.

I've noticed that we constantly categorize our lives, and we have a tendency to maintain control of certain categories. This was certainly true for me in the categories of diet and exercise. We, as Christians, may often think or act as though certain areas of our lives do not qualify when we talk about the Lordship of Christ. I'm not sure we would ever be so bold as to claim this, yet our habits and actions reveal the truth about us when our strongholds press us.

Let me ask you a few questions. Do you truly desire to strive to be everything God wants you to be all the days of your life until you go to Heaven? Can this happen if you withhold particular areas of your life from the Lordship of Christ? Are you willing to daily turn yourself completely over to Him? Do you wish to declare to Jesus, "I am totally Yours—even the strongholds that have been holding me back"? We must answer these questions if we are serious about living the victorious Christian life.

I have reflected at length on a little parabolic illustration that Jesus used to teach a profound truth about a successful spiritual lifestyle. Jesus even related this truth to Himself and His personal spiritual success in John 12:23-24,

> *23 Jesus replied, "Now the time has come for the Son of Man to enter into his glory. 24 I tell you the truth, unless a kernel of wheat is planted in the soil and dies, it remains alone. But its death will produce many new kernels—a plentiful harvest of new lives."*

In the context of this passage, Jesus was talking about fulfilling the will of God for His life by going to the cross. Jesus was actually predicting His death and revealing how He was going to honor and glorify the Father while on earth. Shouldn't this be the desire of everyone who calls themselves by His name? There were some who didn't want Jesus to die, and even the physical and emotional sides of Jesus were troubled at the prospect of what lay ahead at the cross. Notice what He says a few verses later. *27 "Now my soul is deeply troubled. Should I pray, 'Father, save me from this hour'? But this is the very reason I came! 28 Father, bring glory to your name." Then a voice spoke from Heaven, saying, "I have already brought glory to my name, and I will do so again."*

Jesus admitted that the idea of asking the Father to spare Him from death crossed His mind, but He quickly reminded us that He knew He came to die on the cross. In addition, He uttered a prayer that we should all seek to pray concerning our lives. He prayed, "Father, bring glory to your name." Oh, that we would pray this prayer with fervor in every aspect of our lives, especially in the areas of our strongholds! We should understand how penetrating this prayer can be if we apply it to our strongholds. I must pray, "Father, bring glory to Your name, even in the way I eat and exercise." If you will pray this prayer, inserting your stronghold, you will begin to experience victory in your spiritual life.

How was it, then, that Jesus crossed this emotional hurdle and continued toward the Cross? How do we get to the place spiritually where we will pray the prayer Jesus prayed? In order to come to the place where we will allow Jesus to help us overcome our hurdles, we must first look at the illustration He used regarding a simple seed. For Jesus to glorify the Father with His life, He had to be like a seed that is planted in the soil and dies. In other words, the seed had to lose itself and die in order to produce! Jesus taught us a truth from the world of farming that was true in His life as our Savior. Jesus was saying that He could never be who He came to be if He was not willing to die. Furthermore, I believe He taught that this truth not only applied to the **seed** and to **Himself as a Savior**, but also to us as His **Saints**. Therefore, you and I must also die. We now know Jesus literally and physically died, but this is not what He is asking us to do. I believe Jesus is instructing us to do what Paul said about himself in Galatians 2:20, *My old self has been crucified with Christ. It is no longer I who live, but Christ lives in me. So I live in this earthly body by trusting in the Son of God, who loved me and gave himself for me.* We should continue to live, but not for ourselves. After our salvation, we should, on a daily basis, seek to crucify our personal and selfish desires and live for Him. Jesus explained in John 12:25-26, *25 Those who love their life in this world will lose it. Those who care nothing for their life in this world will keep it for eternity. 26 Anyone who wants to be my disciple must follow me, because my servants must be where I am. And the Father will honor anyone who serves me.*

This is truly what the Christian life is meant to be! Here is the problem that arises: in critical areas of our lives, we are not dead to ourselves, but very much alive! We demonstrate this fact daily, and often loudly, through the strongholds in our lives. Let me ask you—how many times does a person have to be saved? Only once! How many times does a person in sanctification have to die to themselves? Every day, and even several times a day! Jesus told us to take up the cross daily and follow Him in Luke 9:23. *Then he said to the crowd, "If any of you wants to be my follower, you must turn from your selfish ways, take up your cross daily, and follow me.*

The cross is not for carrying, but dying. Jesus emphasized that we should die <u>daily</u>! If we are honest, we can see that we all have areas in our lives that still require this death daily.

Some areas may surprise us spontaneously, while others we already know will overtake us. Let me further explain this truth. Recently, I was at a four-way stop in Hendersonville, NC. I was waiting my turn (the person to the right has the right-of-way), when the person to my left took my turn (I think they were from Florida). Before I knew it, I had laid down on my horn—I tried to do it in a Christian way. I was surprised at my own reaction to this situation, especially since this four-way stop is the one right in front of the church where I have served as pastor for 28 years. OUCH! Although my actions in this situation were unanticipated, my propensity to overeat and not exercise was a well-developed pattern with premeditation. I wasn't being overtaken by this sin, as Paul writes about in Galatians 6. No, I was a willing participant. I would often make my plans ahead with eating in mind, and think of how much I would eat. It saddens me to say that I would do this with little thought of any consequences, and I regularly suppressed any conviction about this struggle. Many of you know how easily this pattern develops with your sinful strongholds. It is a habitual pattern. Paul wrote in Romans 6:11 that this pattern should not be part of our Christian lives. *So you also should consider yourselves to be dead to the power of sin and alive to God through Christ Jesus.*

Although I knew it was wrong, this pattern was happening to me regularly in the area of my stronghold. It may still happen to me at times, and perhaps it may also be happening to you. While we are alive in Jesus, we also demonstrate we are very much alive unto ourselves. If you say you are saved and Jesus is living within you, you must answer these questions about your daily lifestyle:

- If you curse, who says that word? You or Jesus?
- If you lust or commit sexual relations outside of marriage, who does this? You or Jesus?

- If you are addicted to alcohol or drugs, who does this? You or Jesus?
- If you steal, who is stealing? You or Jesus?
- If you gossip, who speaks these words? You or Jesus?
- If you overeat and don't exercise, who is responsible for this? You or Jesus?

Of course, we are always responsible for our actions. Jesus wouldn't do any of these things, nor would He lead us to do them. It is only when we daily say "no" to what our flesh desires, and "yes" to Jesus' Lordship, that we will glorify the Father in what we say and do! We must allow Jesus to give us victory over our strongholds!

What happens if we don't? Well, the same thing that happens to an unplanted seed: it simply remains alone, unproductive, and unsuccessful in its purpose. Many people do not even scratch the surface of what they could do if they would just die to themselves, and get out of the way of God's plan. What would happen if we gave up our strongholds? I believe when the Bible says that God will "wipe away our tears," He may be referring to the Judgment Seat of Christ. This is where He reveals to us what our lives could have been if we would have completely surrendered to His Lordship. The Lord has convicted me to address the strongholds in my life while I still have time on earth. I have been praying daily, "Lord, thank You for giving me the opportunity to repent and correct these areas in my life."

I am learning that I don't have to be a glamorous "seed," but simply a seed dead to myself and alive to Jesus. Only then can I produce <u>much</u> for His Kingdom! Have you ever considered the potential of one seed, when this seed is planted and fulfills its purpose? One little dark, crusty watermelon seed can produce a red heart, white rind, and multicolored skin that is almost impossible for even a professional artist to paint. All of this may come about from one seed, dead unto itself. Our potential is unlimited when we are totally surrendered to the Lordship of our Savior. I am learning that God can take even me, a country boy from Chesnee, SC, who pastors a church named Mud Creek, and do great things for His Kingdom. The more people see of Jesus, and the less they see of me (I mean several pound cakes less), the more He will use me, and the more the Father is glorified in my life.

John the Baptist said, "I must decrease and He must increase." These words have a new meaning to me. I now apply those words not only to my spirit and attitude, but also to my body. How I desire for God to be glorified in all I do, including how I deal with the strongholds in my life! Are you interested in this? Today, I feel more alive in Jesus living under His Lordship than at any other time in my 54 years of living. What a feeling! Why don't you join me in this daily discipline? Why not aggressively apply this truth of dying daily to your biggest challenge and obstacle? Why not see just how much you and I can produce in our lives for God's Kingdom by daily dying to self, and being alive only in Jesus Christ?

In salvation, we learn what Jesus does <u>in us</u>. Why not experience all He wants to do <u>through us</u>? I am learning what is written in Romans 14:17, *For the Kingdom of God is not a matter of what we eat or drink, but of living a life of goodness and peace and joy in the Holy Spirit.* There is overwhelming joy if you are in God's will. I have given up things which I thought I couldn't live without; things robbing me of "abundant life." John 15:10-11 reads, *When you obey my commandments, you remain in my love, just as I obey my Father's commandments and remain in his love. 11 I have told you these things so that you will be filled with my joy. Yes, your joy will overflow!*

Jesus clearly taught that our joy is linked to obedience. I must seek and obey Him in every area of my life, and only then will I experience the joy and satisfaction of all Jesus has saved me to be. Jerry Bridges reminds us that "to experience this joy we must make some choices. We must choose to forsake sin, not only because it is defeating us, but because it grieves the heart of God." I have come to understand that when I sin, spontaneously or regularly with a stronghold, I not only disappoint myself and others, but I break the heart of God, who has a much better way of living planned for me! I have come to the place where I am willing to say NO to the fleshly temptation to over-indulge my appetite. Jesus is helping me practice this discipline daily. I know He will also help you if you ask Him. Note God's promises:

Seek his will in all you do, and he will show you which path to take.
Proverbs 3:6

13 No, dear brothers and sisters, I have not achieved it, but I focus on this one thing: Forgetting the past and looking forward to what lies ahead, 14 I press on to reach the end of the race and receive the Heavenly prize for which God, through Christ Jesus, is calling us.
Philippians 3:13-14

God is able, and will do His part in sanctification. I must be willing to accept my responsibility, and daily say "no" to the flesh, the Devil, and the world. As Chuck Colson said in *Loving God*, "Holiness is the every day business of every Christian. It evidences itself in the decisions we make and things we do, hour by hour, and day by day."

With each step of surrender and obedience, the Lord takes me a little further in the journey of spiritual maturity. Would you like to join me? Perhaps the Lord has been speaking to you for some time about an area of your life. Should you take Him seriously? Perhaps an old, anonymous story about a conversation that took place at sea will help us refocus on the only voice we need to hear.

The captain of the ship looked into the dark night and saw faint lights in the distance. Immediately he told his signalman to send a message: "Alter your course 10 degrees south."

Promptly a return message was received: "Alter your course 10 degrees north."

The captain was angered; his command had been ignored. So he sent a second message: "Alter your course 10 degrees south – I am the captain!"

Soon another message was received: "Alter your course 10 degrees north – I am seaman third class Jones."

Immediately the captain sent a third message, knowing the fear it would evoke: "Alter your course 20 degrees south – I am a battleship."

Then the reply came: "Alter your course 10 degrees north – I am a lighthouse."

In the midst of our dark and foggy times, all sorts of voices are shouting orders into the night, telling us what to do, how to adjust our lives. Out of the darkness, one voice signals something quite opposite to the rest – something almost absurd. But the voice happens to be the Light of the World, and we ignore it at our peril.

I want to ask you to take a moment to pray. Ask God to speak to you about anything He wants to change or correct in your life. Please know how much He loves you and cares about what is best for you. Pray something like this:

Dear Lord, I am asking you to speak to my heart. I am open and listening to what you have to say about any area in my life. Lord, I may already know the areas in which you will convict me. However, this time, let Your conviction set in, and let my desire to allow You to change me be genuine. Lord, let this be a new beginning in my life.
    Amen

Steps Back

√   "Do you truly desire to strive to be everything God wants you to be all the days of your life until you go to Heaven? Can this happen if you withhold particular areas of your life from the Lordship of Christ? Are you willing to daily turn yourself completely over to Him?"

√   "The cross is not for carrying, but dying. Jesus emphasized that we should die <u>daily</u>! If we are honest, we can see that we all have areas in our lives that still require this death daily."

Steps Into

√ John 12:24 teaches, *I tell you the truth, unless a kernel of wheat is planted in the soil and dies, it remains alone. But its death will produce many new kernels—a plentiful harvest of new lives.*

Do you realize that daily death to your own desires and strongholds produces spiritual growth and life?

√ John 15:10 reads, *When you obey my commandments, you remain in my love, just as I obey my Father's commandments and remain in his love.*

Because Christ set the example, you also can obey Him and remain in fellowship with Him. Are you right now obeying Him? Would you describe yourself as "remaining in His love?"

Steps Forward

√ What areas of your life are easy for you to submit to the Lord? What areas are hard for you to submit to the Lord? Do you realize the areas where there are strongholds?

√ Do you understand that sanctification is a continual process and not a singular event?

√ What areas in your life are "alive to Christ"? What areas in your life do you need to "die to yourself"?

Chapter 5

Step Toward Purity

Sanctification is the real change in man from the sordidness of sin to the purity of God's image.
William Ames

God blesses those whose hearts are pure, for they will see God.
Matthew 5:8

So far, we have addressed some internal steps to defeating our strongholds—admitting honestly where we struggle, evaluating where we are, finding identity in Christ, and surrendering to His Lordship. Now, I want to show you some practical steps I took to confess and repent of the stronghold I experienced in my life. Even if your stronghold is not the same, please continue to read, because I believe the steps you need to take are very similar. My first step may surprise you: I came to the realization that I needed a <u>check-up</u> from the neck-up. This first step toward purity is winning the battle in your mind. In order to conquer the stronghold that prevents us from being who God wants us to be, we must begin with our mind. Was it possible that my overeating and lack of exercise was a bigger problem with my mind than with my belly? Yes! Strongholds dominate us because in our mind we are either ignorant or rebellious to what God says about sin. Our bodies will always follow our minds.

First, I was ignoring scriptural truth when Jesus said, "It is what comes out of a man's heart that defiles him." In other words, it is not what goes into the man that destroys him, but rather what his thinking was before he ever took anything in. I knew this was true in several areas, such as anger before murder and lust before adultery. However, I never considered that what was really destroying me was not primarily about what I was taking in (too much food). Instead, I came to understand that my struggle was a result of what predicated my actions: my thinking about food in the first place. I knew there were certain thoughts that had no business occupying my mind. For example, I knew that if I lusted after another woman, God would be displeased with me, and Deborah would kill me. My precious wife, Deborah, who plays the organ in our church, has never brought up divorce. She has, a few times, brought up the subject of murder. She has made it abundantly clear that it would be fatal. I therefore knew that it would be wrong and unhealthy to lust for another woman. Why, then, did I not realize that it was wrong to lust after food? The answer was partially from ignorance and primarily from rebellion. The Lord taught me that my failure of overeating basically started in my mind with a lust for food. I more clearly noticed this truth as I have studied the book of James. Have you ever noticed that we are our own biggest problem in temptation?

James 1:14-15 teaches that temptation comes from our own desires leading to sin and eventually death. I never wanted to admit that the thoughts in my mind were the problem. If I had a problem, it wasn't my fault. The problem was obviously hereditary, or vocational, or geographical location (many fat people live in the south). It could even have been the ladies in our church, who can cook so well, and keep bringing their dishes to me. I knew I was becoming physically mature (fat), but surely I wasn't to be blamed. I was truly developing a problem and didn't want to admit it. Until we change our thinking about this issue, we won't be able to do anything about it. In addition, until we agree with what God says about us and our thinking, we won't be able to change.

Like many of you, I did not think I had a problem for quite some time. We always blame someone else. Didn't Adam say that it was the woman, and the woman say it was the serpent? Who was the serpent going to blame? The serpent didn't have a leg left to stand on. According to James, we have no one to blame but ourselves. We are the way we are because of what occurs in our minds. I want you to take a moment and point your index finger toward your brain. Now say, "The biggest problem I face is with my own self in my mind." This is an important first step. Believe it or not, the Devil is not my initial problem—I am! Some of you may be thinking, "Well then, I don't have a problem." But, what if your mind is playing a trick on you by making you think that you don't have a problem? Does the Bible not teach that our thinking can be deceitfully wicked? What if you are operating out of spiritual ignorance and rebellion, and don't even realize it? This is exactly what I was doing! Let me explain. I knew I was overweight by the world's standards, and even by the chart on the wall at the doctor's office. How many times did I sit there finding my height and then my weight? Just for fun, one day I went to my weight first and then my height. The chart said I should be 8' 2" tall. As I mentioned earlier in the book, I joked often that instead of being overweight, I might be under-tall! This was one of my problems. Rarely did I have a serious thought about this stronghold, and I virtually never had a serious spiritual thought about it. As Christians, and especially preachers, we have a way of being very knowledgeable about sins which beset others, while we remain numb or neutral to things that plague us. We are often quiet about these personal issues. This is why you rarely, if ever, hear a sermon on gluttony. Yet 62% of Americans are overweight and 72% of preachers are overweight. Are 62% of the people to whom we preach afflicted this much by any other sin? Are 72% of those of us who preach struggling with any other stronghold as much as overeating and lack of exercise? I think not! I knew I was one of those preachers. I needed to deal with this sin.

You see, I had to admit that I had eating habits which were working against me. I wouldn't each much breakfast, which is the most important meal of the day. I knew one of the reasons I didn't want any breakfast resulted from the late night snacks and meals I consumed. It's not uncommon among preachers to wait until after the church service to eat. And, because I traveled and preached many revivals, I regularly ate on the road late into the evening. Too often, I have sat down to the largest meal of the day after 9:00 pm. My eating habits, coupled with no consistency in exercise, combined to create a dangerous recipe for a crisis in my health. Unfortunately, this recipe can be fatal. As Christians, we can be blind or indifferent to this potential danger. I know I was. I preached the funerals of two close friends, Randy Kilby and Todd Edmiston. Both of these dynamic ministers died prematurely from heart attacks. By their own admission, both overate and exercised too little. God used them both to help awaken me to the reality that I was on the same course of life. I now realize the danger to myself and others. We must allow this dangerous health trend to register with all of us.

Guidestone, who insures 60,000 Southern Baptist staff members, recently reported that 75% of people tested at a recent annual Southern Baptist Convention meeting were overweight or obese by current health standards. Even so, we preachers don't discuss this. As Norman Jameson said, "Gluttony is the only acceptable sin in the Baptist Garden of Eat'n." He's right, and I had fallen into that trap. The first thing I asked God to do was to change my thinking by showing me what His Word said about physical wellness. God clearly revealed His thoughts concerning our bodies:

Dear friend, I hope all is well with you and that you are as healthy in body as you are strong in spirit.
  3 John 2

They are headed for destruction. Their god is their appetite, they brag about shameful things, and they think only about this life here on earth.
  Philippians 3:19

Why had I allowed myself to become so physically unhealthy? Why had I fallen into the sin of idolatry and allowed my appetite for food to become a god? I knew this was not right. I knew I was to love Him with my mind, body, soul, and spirit. The Lordship of Christ should be reflected in all I am and all I do. His Lordship should be evident in how I handle my emotions and how I treat my body. Such evidence did not exist when considering my physical state, and my rebellion was a direct result of my personal thoughts and the battle in my mind. I had to address what I was and wasn't thinking in my mind concerning food and exercise. What I discovered is that sinful strongholds are terribly selfish. Instead of thinking about God and others, I was living for the self-gratification of food. To put it another way, my life revolved around food. My appetite had become a god. This appetite was a controlling factor in my life. I was so selfish, and I did not contemplate how this rebellion was affecting me physically, my ministry, and the people who love and need me!

God is currently teaching me to eat while keeping my family and ministry in mind and with the awareness that I eat in His presence. I now see clearly that when I overate and did not exercise, I wasn't thinking about anyone but myself. I wasn't thinking about God or others. As William White said, "Each time it was a selfish, solitary, sinful act." C. S. Lewis taught that "the medieval thinker linked the sins of gluttony and lust together because both illustrate our frequent failures to control our physical appetites." I am convinced that gluttony, like most sins, is selfish and makes an idol out of food. I was satisfied with the security of my soul, but I didn't give serious thought toward wise, healthy practices for my body, which was in God's service. I doubt anyone would suggest that gluttony would endanger a person's soul, but it certainly was threatening my service for our Lord. I am not alone here! You may even be right where I found myself. If so, why not allow the Lord to change your thinking? One of the first commitments I made was to practice 2 Corinthians 10:5, *We destroy every proud obstacle that keeps people from knowing God. We capture their rebellious thoughts and teach them to obey Christ.*

The Lord has taught me that no thought should go unchecked. Furthermore, He has helped me see the truth of Ecclesiastes 12:14, which causes me to understand that one day at the Judgment Seat of Christ God will judge us for everything—good and bad, secret and public.

The Lord is teaching me to eat in moderation, and He has used wise individuals to teach me how to be healthier when I eat. I want to share one mental exercise that helped me tremendously, even before I began physical exercise. Sam Varner asked me to visualize in my mind the time in my life when I felt the healthiest. As I reflected back, I felt most healthy when I was in college. My weight was down, and I was physically fit. I even sported some Elvis sideburns (they each weighed about a half pound – Elvis would have been so proud). Even with the sideburns, I was at an ideal weight by my doctor's standards. Then, Sam asked me to compare that weight with what I thought Jesus would want me to weigh. Immediately I knew the Lord would want my weight somewhere in the vicinity of 200 pounds—give or take a Twinkie or two. But I immediately reacted, thinking, "There's no way." Why, I would have to lose over 100 pounds! I couldn't do that with my schedule, having to eat out often, and with a wife that cooks as well as Deborah. And what about Doris Waldrop's biscuits? What about Hot Dog World? What about those sweet ladies in the church who bring me cakes? What about the motto I had lived with so long, "When Jesus comes back I don't want there to be an unopened jar of peanut butter in our cabinet!" Actually, He could have come at any day and hour without that happening, unless He came between the time Deborah brought the groceries home and when I had time to take off the lid. Do you see what I was doing? I was exercising wrong thinking. I was simply making excuses. I was blaming my circumstances on others. I was trying to excuse my sin. I completely doubted that I could ever get back to my ideal weight. Shakespeare once said, "Our doubts are traitors and make us lose the good we might win by fearing to ever attempt." Why shouldn't I strive for the best concerning my health? I had strived for the best in every other area of my life. I was blessed with the best wife, the best family, the best church, the best friends, and even a pretty, old Corvette. Why not be in the best health, especially if it were possible? Some people would give anything to be in better health, but physically can't. I could, but I realized that up to that point, I wouldn't. More than once, the thought has crossed my mind that I should be ashamed of how I have allowed my body to become so out of shape. Could I really change? I had made so many New Year's resolutions, mid-year resolutions and late night resolutions, but to no avail. Could I really make a change, and could I stick with it?

With God's help, I made up my mind that I was going to take action and keep my commitment to change. I was going to change my thinking and ask God to make it happen. Doesn't the Bible teach that Jesus can make anything happen? I believe what Jesus said in Mark 9:23, *What do you mean, "If I can?" Jesus asked. "Anything is possible if a person believes."* When I started believing that this could happen, I came to the place where I was absolutely willing to do my part! My part was to surrender every area of my life to Him. I sincerely believe that I won a tremendous battle in my mind. I now understood who God wanted me to become, and I literally still visualize this every day. I have even set a picture on my nightstand of the person I used to be so that I will daily ponder who I want to become. Earl Knightingale said, "Success is best defined by a progressive realization of a worthy goal and ideal." I now have a goal of healthy, abundant living. What is most satisfying is that God has spoken to my heart and said He is pleased with me. Our focus and goal in every area of life should be only to please Him! As Thomas Merton said, "This kind of thinking is not a psychological trick but a theological grace." I believe this truth, and I thank God every day for the opportunity to do something about this stronghold. I now practice healthy eating and daily exercise, and I am learning the art of biblical meditation. This is not what the world teaches, but instead what Isaac practiced in Genesis 24:63: *One evening as he was walking and meditating in the fields."* And like the Psalmist in Psalm 63:6: *I lie awake thinking of you, meditating on you through the night.*

Like Elijah, I am asking God to speak to me in every area of my life loudly or with a still small voice. Lord, I am thinking and listening. James teaches that we are to be quick to listen to what God wants to say to us about any area of our lives. I am learning that God has long desired to speak to me about many things! The Lord is teaching me daily that He wants all of me under His Lordship. God is not only teaching me to listen, but to obey Him. Obedience begins in our minds. I am learning to practice Romans 12:1-2.

1 And so, dear brothers and sisters, I plead with you to give your <u>bodies</u> to God because of all he has done for you. Let them be a living and holy sacrifice—the kind he will find acceptable. This is truly the way to worship him. 2 Don't copy the behavior and customs of this world, but let God transform you into a new person by changing the way you <u>think</u>. Then you will learn to know God's will for you, which is good and pleasing and perfect.

I can see how God is daily molding me into the likeness of His Son. Have you ever considered that becoming more like Jesus may mean one particular commitment in your life, such as losing weight and living a healthier lifestyle? Many like to use the acronym—WWJD—asking, "What would Jesus do?" Why not consider what Jesus ate and how He took care of Himself? I am convinced that Jesus did not go to the cross as an overweight, out of shape Savior. I don't believe that Jesus would ever have failed to take care of Himself. During the time Jesus lived on the earth, Don Colbert believes that "Most people walked from three to ten miles a day." Evangelist Arthur Blessitt once obtained maps showing the roads Jesus traveled. He calculated that the "total miles Jesus walked during the three years of His public ministry were 3,125 miles." Yes, I believe Jesus got plenty of exercise, and I believe He also maintained a healthy diet. Colbert asserts, "Jesus was the perfect role model, wisely consuming whole-grain breads, pure water, and fresh foods that were low in fat, salt, additives and preservatives." Jesus demonstrated perfectly what kind of eating habits we should have, and ate to live rather than lived to eat. How do I know this? Because Jesus lived for His Father and other people, while the glutton does not. Jesus never exaggerated the importance of any one thing the way I exaggerated the importance of food. We should never place what Henry Fairlie called an "inappropriate place and value" on any one thing or person in our lives. This is what sin does! You see, healthy food and exercise are essential to our well-being.

Everything should be done in moderation, including eating! Lust within us tempts us to act and live in excess. Both gluttony and lust take essential parts of life and make them sinful outside the bounds of God's limits. I have no desire to live outside the boundaries God has given me, and in my mind, I daily choose to live within God's limits. This is what I encourage you to do with your stronghold. I guarantee you, regardless of the area in which you struggle, your conflict begins with the desire in your mind to live in excess, outside God's boundaries for you. I am choosing to now live within God's limits in all areas of my life, including in the areas of diet and exercise. Will you also choose this with your stronghold? Exodus 20:3 says, *You must not have any other god but me.* That includes the god of food! I never viewed myself as an idolater, but God revealed to me that food had become an idol in my life. He has broken and humbled me in regard to my affliction. As Hannah Whitall Smith said, "True humility can bear to see its own utter weakness and foolishness revealed." How foolish I have been! I was so dangerous while I lived so carelessly with no regard for my health. The change I have encountered in this area is not a mid-life crisis, but simply a spiritual wake-up. God has clearly revealed to me the truth that sin of any kind is wrong, dangerous, and has no place in the Christian life! Whether it is my stronghold or yours – it's sin! Lamentations 3:40 states, *Instead, let us test and examine our ways. Let us turn back to the Lord.* And, as 1 John 1:8-9 teaches, we must confess our sin to the Lord, and resolve not to continue in our sinful ways. John Burroughs said, "Nothing relieves and ventilates the mind like a resolution." Here is a prayer I prayed and continue to pray:

Lord, I want to confess to You that in the areas of diet and exercise, I have sinned and come short of your glory. I am sorry, Lord. You, my family, and my church have deserved better, and for this I am also sorry. You have deserved better than an overweight, out of shape Greg Mathis. I promise You, my family, and my church a healthier, leaner lifestyle. With Your help, Lord, I surrender to Your Lordship over my life. I will continue to take steps to correct this wrong. I trust Your Word.

Dear Lord, with Your help, I resolve to be a healthier person. Lord, You have changed my thinking, and now in repentance I commit to change my ways. Lord, I pray that you will allow me to influence others who look upon my life. I hope they see that I truly love You with my mind, body, and soul. Lord, never let me forget that if I am not loving you completely, it will first be obvious through an overweight, out of shape body. Lord, may all areas of my life be completely surrendered to Your Lordship.

Amen

Steps Back

√ "According to James, we have no one to blame but ourselves. We are the way we are because of what occurs in our minds. I want you to take a moment and point your index finger toward your brain. Now say, 'The biggest problem I face is with my own self in my mind.' This is an important first step."

√ "I have no desire to live outside the boundaries God has given me, and in my mind, I daily choose to live within God's limits. This is what I encourage you to do with your stronghold. I guarantee you, regardless of the area in which you struggle, your conflict begins with the desire in your mind to live in excess, outside God's boundaries for you. I am choosing to now live within God's limits in all areas of my life."

Steps Into

√ 2 Corinthians 10:5 says, *We destroy every proud obstacle that keeps people from knowing God. We capture their rebellious thoughts and teach them to obey Christ.*

Do you realize that your greatest war is in your mind? Would you say that you capture your thoughts and bring them under Christ's Lordship?

√ 1 John 1:9 teaches, *But if we confess our sins to him, he is faithful and just to forgive us our sins and to cleanse us from all wickedness.*

The first step towards purity of thought is confession. Are you regularly confessing your thoughts to God? If you are unsure how to begin, look back at the prayer concluding this chapter.

Steps Forward

√ Who is winning the battle within your mind? You or God?

√ Do you believe that if our thoughts do not reflect Jesus, our actions will not reflect Jesus either? Would you say that your thoughts are reflecting more of you or more of Jesus?

√ Write down some of the thoughts connected to your stronghold. Commit this week to "capture" those thoughts each time they enter your mind. I have found that I can turn my thoughts to Jesus by praying or meditating on Scripture.

Chapter 6

Step Toward Discipline

In reading the lives of great men, I found that the first victory they won was over themselves...self-discipline with all of them came first.
Harry S. Truman

I discipline my body like an athlete, training it to do what it should. Otherwise, I fear that after preaching to others I myself might be disqualified.
1 Corinthians 9: 27

When it comes to thinking about our physical health, we need to know that a sin-filled world makes healthy living difficult for us. We need to understand that our bodies are deteriorating and dying. This is actually a process that begins at birth. From the moment we were born, we began to die. This reality is a consequence of the sinful fall of Adam and Eve. Even with an excellent diet and disciplined exercise routine, our body will <u>still</u> deteriorate and die. An older man in our church says when he sees someone jogging, "He is just trying to outrun death." This is why the Bible says we should put more emphasis on our spiritual health than our physical health. 1 Timothy 4:8-9 reads, *8 Physical exercise has some value, but spiritual exercise is much more important, for it promises a reward in both this life and the next. 9 This is true, and everyone should accept it.*

Although spiritual health should be the larger interest in our lives, scripture does not say that physical exercise is of no value. When you hear someone remark, "Oh, there is no point to exercise and eat right," nothing could be further from the truth. Now, I understand clearly that while I am on this earth, my body is subject to a number of diseases. This is a consequence of Adam and Eve's sin. I also know that as a Christian, my body belongs to the Lord, and He may do what He pleases with it. According to 1 Corinthians 6:19-20, I am God's temple and belong to Him.

I believe the Lord desires us to trust Him to do whatever He wants with our bodies. If God wants to place my body in a hospital bed, He can. If He wants these feet to go to the mission field, I should go. If He wants these eyes to have a vision for the world, I should witness. If He wants this mouth to preach the Gospel, or these hands to feed the poor, I should be willing and obey. We should all be willing! This is easier said than done, but God wants all of us to have this level of dedication and commitment to Him. If God allows an affliction to attack my body, while I may not understand it, I should trust His sovereignty and wisdom and accept this situation in faith. Examine the life of Billy Graham, whom I have admired for years, as an example. He has suffered for some time with Parkinson's disease. While I don't understand why he has suffered, I trust God, as Dr. Graham does, for His will to be done, even though it may be mysterious.

I want to share an important truth God has taught me on this journey. A great difference exists between the tests in life that come from God and the self-inflicted wounds I bring on myself. I am concerned that many problems we experience in life, even physical issues, are self-inflicted. I used to have high blood pressure, and God revealed to me that this was my own fault. Although this was the case for me and my health, I do realize that this is not always the case for everyone. For a time, I was experiencing many health problems that were self-inflicted, including the entrance into a potential early grave. God told me that if He desired to send or allow a sickness to come into my life, He was able do this without my help. He impressed on me that He wasn't ready for my body to have a heart attack, stroke, or diabetes. He may allow any of these things to happen at a later time, but He would be appreciative if I would straighten up and take better care of myself. He also clearly revealed to me that the areas in my life that needed the most improvement were the areas of my eating habits and daily exercise. Why these areas? Because these were the most severe, sinful strongholds in my life, and they stood in the way of His Lordship. I was most disobedient in these areas. The Lord was exposing the point of my greatest rebellion. He was asking me to demonstrate my sincerity in my personal relationship with Him. As I ministered, He wanted me healthy, strong, energetic, and totally disciplined to His calling in my life. He wanted me to show His Lordship in my life in an obvious way, so that people would easily and clearly notice. He wanted my preaching to be powerful, convicting, and an example to others. How could I possibly minister to others and help them remove the speck from their eye if I was not willing to get rid of the log (that would be a Stuckey's Pecan Log Roll with cream) in my own eye (or mouth)? I certainly understood His message, and I am praying you will also understand.

I am not perfect, and never will be this side of Heaven, but God certainly expected more discipline than I demonstrated. Someone said the other day, "Well, none of us are perfect, so my imperfection is going to be in the area of eating." This was much like my own thought process, but God has since convicted me of this careless, excuse-making mentality. The most frightening thing about my stronghold is that I did not address it for so long and allowed so much time to go by. I beg you to allow God to speak to you in the area of your stronghold before it is too late. This will begin with conviction, then confession, followed with a course of correction. To correct the area of your stronghold, you must have a plan of attack.

Someone said, "It is possible that a man could live twice as long if he didn't spend the first half of his life acquiring habits that shorten the other half." Without a doubt, I had developed some dangerously bad habits when it came to eating and exercise. I basically ate everything I wanted (and more) and never seriously exercised. I can honestly say that until recent months I never combined healthy eating with daily exercise. Now don't get me wrong, I had lost weight before. Through the years I have lost and gained enough weight to make a fair-sized basketball team. The team would not be very tall, but they would surely be able to post up and block out (short, thick players can do that). Believe it or not, I actually played basketball in high school. My coach once said, "Greg, I am not sure your body was made for a basketball uniform." He was right. I was physically better built for football, and experienced some success in that sport. Like many people who played sports, the older I get, the better I remember I was. Even to this day, I wonder what might have happened if I would have played that sport at an ideal weight. I trained with effort, but never exercised good eating habits.

I believe that our young people would be blessed if we, as adults, would stress healthy eating and proper exercise early in their lives, whether or not they participate in sports. Current statistical reports about childhood obesity are alarming. Too often, children spend much of their time in front of televisions and computers while eating junk food and not exercising. As a result, the number of overweight teens and children has tripled in previous years. According to the U.S. Surgeon General, "If a child is overweight there is a 70% chance he will be overweight as an adult. The percentage increases to 80% if one or more parents are overweight." Obesity is a crisis in this country. This crisis must be corrected, beginning with parents and role models, <u>particularly preachers</u>. I have spent my entire time in ministry urging young people not to drink, smoke, or have sexual relations outside of marriage. I have not, however, stood one time in the pulpit and urged them not to overeat. I could not because of my poor personal example. Let me ask you, does the Devil care what he uses to destroy us? Does he get greater joy from alcohol and immoral sex than from gluttony? I wouldn't even begin to tell you that I know how the Devil thinks, but I wonder if he isn't belly laughing at us about how subtly he attacks us in the area of obesity. All the Devil desires to do is destroy us. Peter says in 1 Peter 5:8, *Be self-controlled and alert. Your enemy the Devil prowls around like a roaring lion looking for someone to devour.*

The Devil would be just as content to destroy us at an "all you can eat" buffet as he would at a liquor store or house of prostitution. The Devil attacks us in our areas of weakness and fleshly desires. Primarily, my weakness has been food. I know many reading this book need a change in this area just as much as I did, and may even be reaching a point of desperation. How can we overcome these weaknesses? We must have a plan of attack against our strongholds. As God helps us realize spiritually what has occurred within us and how sinful our strongholds are, we must also have a practical plan of attack. Conviction is not enough. Paul says in Ephesians 6 that we must be prepared because we are up against far more than we can handle on our own. We must demonstrate confession, commitment, and then follow a correct course of action.

I want to share with you what God has taught me through my friend, Sam Varner. Sam is the author of *Slimmer, Younger, Stronger*, a book I highly recommend you read. He is a former Strength and Conditioning Coach for the United States Olympic Team. While Sam's program has helped many athletes win gold medals, God has used him to help me personally strive for the spiritual goal of exercising some strict self-control. The goal I am after reaches far beyond my physical body to something more spiritual. I have, for many months, been physically disciplining my body so that my ministry on earth would not be cut short. Sam's program consists of some simple steps to achieve optimum health. This program has certainly worked for me, as I have now lost over 100 pounds. I echo the words from the great Olympic gold-medal skier, Picabo Street: "Most importantly, Sam has taught me that the mind, body, and spirit are equally essential to good health." I am privileged to be Sam's pastor, but God has humbled me to allow Sam to be my mentor on my journey to greater physical health. God has used Sam to coach me in this endeavor. Sam quickly deflects any praise to God, but I am acutely aware of how God has used Sam in my life.

This process began when Sam brought his new wife, Kathy, to meet me. I knew Sam's background and reputation, and that he is nationally known in the fields of nutrition, health, and fitness. Therefore, I asked him to give me a few tips—not sirloin tips with rice and gravy—about how I might lose a few pounds before my son Jared's wedding, which was only three weeks away. I actually wanted to be able to button my coat for the pictures. He offered me some sound advice, and then asked me if I had any serious interest to do more than temporarily lose a few pounds. I believe God arranged that meeting on that day. I know now that this meeting had very little to do with being introduced to his lovely new wife (I mean no offense to you, Kathy), but it was God offering me a <u>way out</u> of my stronghold.) God was doing no less than what he promised in 1 Corinthians 10:13, *No temptation has seized you except what is common to man. And God is faithful; he will not let you be tempted beyond what you can bear. But when you are tempted, he will also <u>provide a way out</u> so that you can stand up under it.*

I am confident that I had many chances before this opportunity to address this issue, but something was different about this particular time and situation. God had always been able, but I wasn't willing. I was now willing! I pray that those reading this book would be ready to join me in this willingness toward wellness. Sam offered me one year of his life if I would give him one year of my life to strongly attack the strongholds of overeating and lack of exercise. I agreed, and the journey began. The basic principles of this path apply to any stronghold, and if the problem you experience is not overeating, please continue to read on. Simply apply these disciplines in addressing your stronghold.

Discipline # 1

Oddly, Sam didn't begin with a certain diet or exercise program. Now don't misunderstand, Sam did not give me permission to follow the Little Debbie truck to the grocery store. (Have you ever tried replacing the cream out of their oatmeal cakes with peanut butter? I'm sorry, just a lingering thought.) My coach began by addressing the thoughts in my mind, and requested that I daily ask the Lord to change my thinking. I began to understand that so much of how we act as individuals is mental and habitual. I first had to decide in my mind what was right in the Lord's sight for me, and then focus on these facts. My mother taught me that if I would count to ten before I said anything this might make a difference in what words were spoken from my mouth. Sam was teaching me to spend time considering what I would (or should) and would not (or should not) eat. If I could simply spend time pondering this, perhaps I would realize that certain foods were not good for me. Now that I have been actually thinking about what I eat, several people have tried to assist me by pointing out what they thought I could or could not have. Let me pause and correct a misconception about this program. My coach said, "Greg you can have anything you want." I thought, "Hallelujah—I want to go to Hot Dog World!" (If you have never been there you owe it to yourself to try it.) Then Sam added a condition. I had to spend time thinking before I had "anything I wanted" and consider how much I would eat. I had never done this before. Honestly, it would often be a chore to take a moment and pray before attacking a Big Mac. Have you ever noticed how we, as Americans (especially Southern Baptist preachers), attack our food? If several preachers are present at a buffet line, look out. I needed to slow down and consider what I was about to eat. I needed not only to thank God for the food, but pause and ask Him how much of it He truly wanted me to have. I started changing my thoughts from how much food I wanted and how tasty the food would be, to whether or not the food was healthy, and would this food prevent me from physically being who God wants me to be. I reversed the emotional impact of overeating. I used to first overeat and then experience guilt as a result. I now instead choose to think about my actions ahead of time, and feel those emotions before I eat my food.

Why not consider ahead of time how you and I are going to feel after we act, and how our actions hurt and interrupt our journey toward physical and spiritual health? I learned to visualize an image of myself at my ideal weight, and then gaze at the honey bun in my hand and ask myself whether or not eating this food is what is best for me. Do I want some of it, half of it, all of it, or perhaps, after thinking about it, I really don't want any of it. What a tremendous difference this exercise has made in my life! I now understand that if I will spend time pondering my health and God's will for my life, His purpose for me will be more meaningful than any meal, snack, or item in the food chain. My love for food and eating is waning, while my love for God's will concerning my health and life is growing. This is a crucially important first step to success! This exercise must be applied to your stronghold on a daily basis.

Discipline # 2

Learn to read food labels. Eating healthy does not mean starvation. I currently eat enough and am not constantly hungry, but I eat the right foods. I have eliminated from my diet fried foods, desserts, white bread, and unhealthy snacks. I eat a good amount of vegetables, salads, grilled chicken, fish, fruit, and raw nuts. This diet is very similar to other practical diets being promoted today. I drink a significant amount of water daily. I only drink water, skim milk, and 100% juice. I have even eliminated soft drinks that are artificially sweetened. I have learned that artificial sweeteners aren't good for us because they actually stimulate our appetites. If I want a snack, I eat healthy Kashi bars and Cliff bars, which you will be able to find at most any grocery store. Sam has showed me that a healthy snack must contain at least 3 grams of dietary fiber (read the label on the back). I eat whole wheat, whole grain bread, and nothing processed or enriched. Here is a sample of what I eat daily:

Suggested Daily Menu

Breakfast
    2 eggs
    Sliced tomatoes
    Whole wheat toast with butter and jelly
    A glass of skim milk

Mid-Morning Snack
    Kashi or Cliff bar
    1 piece of fruit

Lunch
    Lean Deli Sandwich on Whole Wheat (no mayo)
    A pickle
    10 – 12 Terra chips (made without preservatives)
    Water to drink

Mid-afternoon snack
    Kashi or Cliff bar
    1 piece of fruit

Dinner
    Grilled Chicken or Fish
    Sweet Potato (little butter & brown sugar)
    Salad (Paul Newman's dressings are the healthiest)

The 8.0 Plan

Sam also taught me another important principle to practice daily, an eating plan that follows a simple path from 8 to 0.

8. Eat only to an 8 on a 1 to 10 fullness scale at every meal. Avoid overeating or eating to complete fullness.

7. Take a wellness sabbatical every 7 days. In other words break your routine every 7 days.
6. Get at least 6 net glasses of water everyday. Net means getting enough water to compensate any diuretic or water-siphoning drinks like caffeine or sugary soft drinks.
5. Get at least 5 servings of fruits & vegetables a day.
4. Get at least 4 servings of protein-rich foods. Try to eat some protein-rich food with every meal.
3. Get around 3 servings of healthy whole grains per day. Whole grains have at least 3 grams of fiber per serving.
2. Get at least 2 servings of healthy-fat foods like olives, olive oil, avocados, nuts and seeds.
1. Get no more than 1 serving of "junk foods" or processed carbohydrates a day. Junk food includes sweets, pastries, soft drinks, candy, cakes, ice cream, artificial sweeteners, etc...
0. Abstain from food 2-3 hours before your regular bedtime.

He also taught me that I should go to bed hungry. He said, "This is how your body burns fat during the night." Hey, if I can lose weight while I sleep, I'm all for it!

The main goal of this eating plan is to eat healthier foods in moderate portions. I have no second helpings of any food (even food that is healthy).

Discipline # 3

You must exercise daily. This may be an area where many of you are tempted to stop reading this book, thinking you can't, won't, or don't have time. I didn't think I had enough time, and I made every imaginable excuse. I finally came to the conclusion that exercise is an important part of healthy living, and I had to make time for it. When you examine the construction of the body, God clearly designed it for movement and exercise. For those of us who do not have jobs that require any physical labor, we must plan a specific time each day to exercise our body. Because I was so busy all day with a constant, unexpected schedule as a minister, I realized my allotted time to exercise would have to be early. I needed my exercise time to be similar to my Bible study time. If I didn't accomplish it early, then I wouldn't get it done. I began to set aside 5:00 – 6:00 AM every morning for exercise (yes, that's early, but it was available). If I was serious about this, I had to do it. I now exercise consistently six days a week, whether I am in town or traveling. This is a time which I have committed to the Lord to discipline my body. I view it as His time, set aside for this purpose. I have found exercising to be addictive and a great habit to add to my list of other life habits. I do a combination of weights and cardio. Listed below is an example:

Suggested Fitness Program

Day 1 Rotation
　　Warm-up, 5 to 10 minutes
　　Medicine Ball Cross Chops, 10 Reps Each Side
　　Leg Curl, 10 Reps
　　Medicine Ball Frontal Chops, 10 Reps Each Side
　　Medicine Ball Reverse Lunges, 10 Reps Each Side
　　V-Squats, 10 Reps
　　Lunge Walks, 10 Reps Each leg
　　Go Thru Circuit 3 Times
　　Cool-down, 2 to 5 minutes STRETCH

Day 2 Rotation
　　Warm-up, 5 to 10 minutes
　　Elliptical Trainer: 12 minute intervals

Sprint 30 seconds every 2 minutes
Treadmill 12 minute intervals
Sprint 30 seconds every 2 minutes
Stair Climber: 6 minute intervals
Sprint 30 seconds every 2 minutes
Cool-down, walk 2 to 5 minutes

Day 3 Rotation
Warm-up, 5 to 10 minutes
Chest Press (machine), 10 Reps
Medicine Ball Frontal Chops, 10 Reps Each Side
Lat. Pull down (underhand grip), 10 Reps
Shoulder Press (machine), 10 Reps
Medicine Ball Crunches on Ball, 10 Reps
Biceps Curls, 10 Reps
Medicine Ball Cross Chops, 10 Reps Each Side
Triceps Pushdown, 10 Reps
Go Thru Circuit 3 Times
Cool-down, 2 to 5 minutes

Day 4 Rotation
Warm-up, 5 to 10 minutes
Elliptical Trainer: 12 minute intervals
Sprint 30 seconds every 2 minutes
Treadmill 12 minute intervals
Sprint 30 seconds every 2 minutes
Stair Climber: 6 minute intervals
Sprint 30 seconds every 2 minutes
Cool-down, walk 2 to 5 minutes
(Pictures, diagrams, and instructions for these and other exercises are available at www.livingwellnessministries. com.)

Sam says we must change our routine about every six weeks to keep our bodies guessing. Trust me, my body has definitely been guessing! It's been guessing what happened to the double cheeseburgers. It's been guessing what happened to the fried peanut butter and banana sandwiches (in memory of Elvis). It's been guessing what I am doing dragging this body to the Pump House Workout Center every morning at 5:00 AM. My body wonders if I have lost my mind. Someone said, "You need to shock your body." If this is true, I have certainly accomplished it. My body has been asking what happened to its time in the recliner. What happened to all the trips to Hot Dog World? My body even suggested that those who worked in the restaurants I frequented may have thought I died, or at least lost my mind. No, I hadn't lost my mind, but I did regain control of my body. I am seeing tremendous results, and not only do I feel better about myself, but I think God, my family, and friends are pleased with the results. My wife Deborah says, "We are going on a second honeymoon!" I am all for that! My daughter says she now sees the daddy she saw when she was a little girl. I feel invigorated, energized, healthy, and fit to minister as long as God would have me serve. Charles Jones said, "Five years from now, you will be pretty much the same as you are today, except for two things: the books you read and the people you get close to." I would like to think in five years I will be a much better and healthier person. This change would be a result of what I have read, learned, and those individuals to whom I have grown close. I am praying God will use this book to help you become a better, healthier person as well! Like you, I have been there. I have experienced many of the feelings and emotions you are experiencing. God helped me, and I promise He will help you. Read what the Bible says about Abraham in Romans 4:20-21: *Abraham never wavered in believing God's promise. In fact, his faith grew stronger, and in this he brought glory to God. 21 He was fully convinced that God is able to do whatever he promises.*

God promises to help us. We don't have to walk and exercise on this journey alone. I love the following poem,

> Faith, simple faith, the promise sees
> And looks to God alone;
> Laughs at impossibilities
> And cries, "It shall be done."

Planning your course of action is vitally important.

- Ask God to change your thinking.
- Ask God to guide you in a sensible course of action, attacking your stronghold. Adopt a disciplined plan and commit to it.
- Know that God is able to do anything. You must simply be willing to let Him help you. He won't ask you to do anything He won't give you the strength to do.

Confucius said, "A man who does not think and plan long ahead will find trouble right at his door." Who is that knocking at your door? Could it be God knocking at the door of your stronghold? Why not sit down, think, pray, and ask God what He wants? I did this, and God revealed to me, "Greg, you have had trouble in this area long enough. Seek Me!" *Trust in the LORD with all your heart and lean not on your own understanding; 6 in all your ways acknowledge him, and he will make your paths straight. Proverbs 3:5-6* My path was straight to the gym and away from the buffet. Patrick Morley said, "We all do exactly what we decide to do. We are the sum of our decisions." Even if you decide to do nothing, you are making a decision. God loved me too much to allow me to stay the way I was. Believe me, He loves you too much to leave you where you are! I think God loved you enough to lead me to write this book. Perhaps

He is using me to help you. This is an opportunity for help. Are you willing? I am willing, and I never doubt that God is more than able.

Steps Back

√ "I want to share an important truth God has taught me on this journey. A great difference exists between the tests in life that come from God and the self-inflicted wounds I bring on myself. I am concerned that many problems we experience in life, even physical issues, are self-inflicted."

√ "Patrick Morley said, 'We all do exactly what we decide to do. We are the sum of our decisions.' Even if you decide to do nothing, you are making a decision."

Steps Into

√ 1 Corinthians 9:27 teaches, *I discipline my body like an athlete, training it to do what it should. Otherwise, I fear that after preaching to others I myself might be disqualified.*

Paul was concerned that without disciplining his body, he could disqualify himself spiritually. Do you realize that you could disqualify yourself spiritually without disciplining your body?

√ Peter says in 1 Peter 5:8, *Be self-controlled and alert. Your enemy the Devil prowls around like a roaring lion looking for someone to devour.*

Would you describe yourself as "self-controlled" with your body? Would your family describe you as self-controlled?

Steps Forward

√ How many of your problems in life have been self-inflicted?

√ Is God knocking at your heart's door saying you have struggled with this long enough?

√ Do you truly believe that God can and will provide you a way out from under your stronghold? Are you willing to intentionally and strategically discipline your body to defeat it?

Chapter 7

A Step Toward Accountability

The best mirror is an old friend.
George Herbert

Confess your sins to each other and pray for each other so that you may be healed. The earnest prayer of a righteous person has great power and produces wonderful results.
James 5:16

W hen I started the journey of aggressively addressing my stronghold, I knew I could not do this alone. I certainly had to do my part by allowing God to work in me, because God never forces anything upon us. God is too much of a gentleman to ever assert, "I am going to do this in your life, whether you want me to or not." Perhaps some of you have been thinking, "I wish God would do something in this area of my life." Because God desires us to be willingly submissive to Him, He will not force us in salvation or sanctification. We have to come to the point where we are willing to follow Him. We must allow Him to do what only He can do. God will help us conform to the image of His Son. This transformation is a gift He offers us spiritually in our lives from beginning to end. It was the apostle Paul who suggested that as Christians, we are really becoming His masterpiece. The Lord has been teaching me about the importance of other people in this process. We must place ourselves around people who will influence us in the right way. For many years, I have preached that the Devil will use three things to ruin us:

- The people we spend time with
- The places we go
- The practices we participate in

To successfully change, you must surround yourself with the right people, go to the right places, and practice right living. When God saves us, He desires us to surround ourselves with people of positive spiritual influence. Such people can and will influence us in a powerful way. We must find others who live the right way, surround ourselves with them, and follow their lead. As a pastor, I strive to be a person of positive influence. I often consider the words from this poem,

My life shall touch a dozen lives
Before this day is done.
Leave countless marks of good or ill,
E'er sets the evening sun.
This, the truth I always wish
The prayer I always pray:
Lord, may my life help other lives
It touches by the way.

I thank God for opportunities to influence others. The problem in my life was that I had an area of weakness where I was a <u>poor influence</u>. I heard no one else say that they wanted to be my size and follow my exercise plan, except a few of my "physically mature" preacher friends. When I was elected President of the North Carolina Baptist Convention, one news reporter described me by writing, "He is physically mature, he likes to listen to Elvis, and he looks like Santa Claus." Most of that was true (I didn't have a white beard). I was big! I needed to change, and in order to change, I needed accountability.

I strongly suspect that if you are struggling with a stronghold, you also need accountability. Dealing with a stronghold is not only difficult, but nearly impossible to overcome alone. This is why many of you are still struggling, and you have yet to conquer your stronghold. Strongholds are complex and challenging! God uses others to help us overcome these struggles. One individual that may help us is a counselor who is knowledgeable in the area of our stronghold. A good Christian counselor can be crucial to your success in overcoming your stronghold. Another individual may be someone who has already walked down your difficult path, and God has helped them overcome their struggle. I seek to be one such person, and I am asking God to use me in your life. God has already used people like Sam Varner and many others in my life.

I have discovered that a very effective tool in my life is my weekly meeting with an accountability group—Jim Frady, W.C. Hare, Cliff McCraw, Tom Owens, Lance Plyler, and Todd Overgaard. You may ask, "What is that?" It's a group of people who meet regularly and hold each other accountable to what they collectively confess they are striving to do. This has been a key ingredient in living the "abundant" Christian life God has for me. I chose these six men in our church, and we meet together on a weekly basis. They hold me accountable and help me follow through with my aggressive attack on my stronghold. I can't tell you how positively this has affected me. Louie Giglio gave a profound definition of the function of an accountability group. He said, "An accountability group is a place where you are consistently candid, open, honest, and vulnerable concerning your potential and actual shortcomings and failures in an atmosphere of mutual love, trust, acceptance, and challenge toward the goal of being conformed to the image of Christ and finishing the race."

This group isn't just about helping me, but helping one another. This is actually a biblical concept. Ephesians 4:9-10 teaches that Jesus came into our world—He descended to us. Jesus came to help us, save us from ourselves, and hold us accountable. The story of Christmas is how Jesus came to earth to help us. Eugene Peterson said that "He moved into our neighborhood" to help. Have you allowed Him to do this for you? Are you willing to allow Jesus to assemble some caring individuals around you to help you with your problem? Could this be a key missing ingredient in your effort to be more like Christ? I believe it is. I need someone to check on me, ask me difficult questions about how I am doing, and remind me of what I have committed to do. There is an old saying, "If you can never inspect, then you can't expect." I believe personal failure can be instant and abrupt, but most often, failure evolves over a period of time. As Christians, we need someone looking out for what is in our best interest. Many of us experienced this type of person in one or both of our parents as we grew into adulthood. However, after we became adults, we have rarely had to give an account to anyone. We are ultimately accountable to God, but as I journey through my life, I need some good friends to hold me accountable, help me understand my confessed weaknesses, and seek what God wants me to do to change.

Getting started may be easy, but the follow-through is difficult. One reason that an accountability group can be so beneficial to our success is because our sin tries to separate us from God, the ones we love, and even church. I have often said, "Show me a person who no longer wants to be in church or around their family, and I will show you someone who has sin dominating their lives." It is dangerous to separate ourselves from others. Proverbs 21:17 reads, *As iron sharpens iron, so a friend sharpens a friend.*

What did Paul mean when he encouraged young Timothy to seek holiness with others in his second letter to him in 2:22? *Run from anything that stimulates youthful lusts. Instead, pursue righteous living, faithfulness, love, and peace. Enjoy the companionship of those who call on the Lord with pure hearts.*

And notice what Scripture teaches in these following passages:

And further, submit to one another out of reverence for Christ.
        Ephesians 5:21

Share each other's burdens, and in this way obey the law of Christ.
        Galatians 6:2

Confess your sins to each other and pray for each other so that you may be healed.
        James 5:16

Don't all of these verses point to accountability with one another? Gordon MacDonald, a highly effective Christian author, made this statement after an unfortunate, immoral failure on his part concerning an inappropriate relationship. He said, "I now realize I was lacking in mutual accountability through personal relationships. We need friendships where one man regularly looks another man in the eye and asks hard questions about our moral life, our lusts, our ambitions, our ego." The well known evangelist Jimmy Swaggart confessed after his embarrassing, immoral failure, "I fasted and I prayed and I begged God for deliverance from pornography. I realize now if I had turned to my brothers in Christ for help, I would have been delivered." Chuck Swindoll stated, "When I learn of someone's spiritual defection or moral fall...I ask, 'Was the person accountable to anyone on a regular basis?' Without exception—without a single exception—the answer has been the same: 'NO!'" It is vitally important to gather ourselves in a group where we can regularly be accountable to each other, especially in areas where we struggle!

I meet every Wednesday afternoon with my accountability partners. I asked my accountability group and prayer partners to check on me and ask me if I have been exercising and eating healthy food. I want them to hold me accountable to do the very things I have conveyed to them that I know God wants me to do. I want them to encourage and exhort me every day to be conformed into the image of Christ. I want them to remind me of His Lordship and my responsibility to surrender to it daily.

Here are several ways that will encourage you to allow others to help you address your problem:

- Don't surround yourself with people who have the same moral failure. They will inevitably pull you down.
- Seek out a godly pastor or counselor and talk honestly and openly about your problem.
- Seek a proven approach to aggressively attack your stronghold. I use Sam Varner's "Twelve Simple Principles to Optimum Health." There are many proven programs to help address various strong-

holds. I strongly suggest that any approach you take be Christian in its orientation. Ultimately, Christ is the answer! I only want to associate myself with tools and individuals that are Christ-oriented. What I like about Sam Varner's approach toward physical and spiritual wellness is that it is Christ-centered.

- Ask a number of people to be your prayer partners in your pursuit to live a life more pleasing to God. The more people you have praying, the better you will be. The truth of James 5:16 rings true, *The fervent prayer of a righteous man availeth much. (KJV)*

- Develop an accountability group of trustworthy, caring, Godly people to meet with you regularly and hold you accountable in your endeavor. It's an awesome experience to share openly and honestly what God is doing in your life. You can be a tremendous encouragement to one another, and if you stray, you will have someone ready to lovingly correct you. Notice Hebrews 3:13, *You must warn each other every day, while it is still "today," so that none of you will be deceived by sin and hardened against God.* And 1 Thessalonians 5:11, *So encourage each other and build each other up, just as you are already doing.* And remember Proverbs 27:5-6, *5 An open rebuke is better than hidden love! 6 Wounds from a sincere friend are better than many kisses from an enemy.*

- Daily read God's Word and pray for strength and guidance. Bible Study is God's way of talking to you. Prayer is your way of talking to God.

- Be willing to invest the necessary time and effort needed to assure you spiritual victory. Discipline is not an option, but a must. It will involve time and sacrifice.

- Journal along the way. This is similar to keeping a diary. Write down your thoughts, temptations, struggles, victories, and challenges. God will use this to reveal to you how He is working in your life. Journaling will become a blessing to you as you reflect back on what you have written. God will use it to remind you of what He has done.

Patrick Morley wrote an interesting statement in his book, *The Man in the Mirror*, when he said,

> *Some men have spectacular failures where in an instant they abruptly burst into flames, crash, and burn. But the more common way men get into trouble evolves from hundreds of tiny decisions – decisions which go undetected – that slowly, like water tapping on a rock, wear down a man's character. Not blatantly or precipitously, but subtly, over time, we get caught in a web of cutting corners and compromise, self-deceit, and wrong thinking, which goes unchallenged by anyone in our lives.*

Surely a group of loving, caring people can help us avoid this. My friends, family, prayer partners, and my accountability group are helping me, challenging me, encouraging me, exhorting me, and expecting me to stay on course and finish the journey God has placed before me. What a blessing these people are to my life! Proverbs 13:20 reads, *Walk with the wise and become wise; associate with fools and get in trouble.* It is vitally important that we surround ourselves with good, godly people. I am fortunate to be around some of the best. Words cannot express how much they mean to me.

Napoleon Hill said, "You can't change where you started, but you can change the direction you are going." I am certainly headed in a far better direction than where I have been in the area of my health. I could not even begin to battle my stronghold without God and the people He has placed in my life. Charles Spurgeon said, "Friendship is one of the sweetest joys of life. Many might have failed beneath the bitterness of their trials had they not found a friend." I want to sincerely thank God for the wonderful people He has placed in my life, and I pray for this blessing of friendship in your life. Henry Ford once said, "My best friends are the ones who bring out the best in me." Thank you, my dear family and friends, for helping me become a better person. Thank you, God, for loving me enough to give me friends who not only love me, but also lovingly correct me. It has been said, "Wise is the man who fortifies his life with friendships." I now understand the wisdom in forming an accountability group, and this group continues to be a blessing in my life. I plan to continue this practice for the rest of my life. I believe that gathering others around you who can help you would certainly be a step in the right direction as you try to overcome your stronghold. Someone said, "The friends that are really worth having are the ones who will listen to your deepest hurts and feel that they are his too." You cannot read the Bible without noticing how important relationships and fellowship are to God's children. Hebrews 10:25 warns us not to neglect gathering together: *And let us not neglect our meeting together, as some people do, but encourage one another, especially now that the day of his return is drawing near.*

It is important to surround yourself with those who have the same biblical approach to life. You should have the Bible as your authority, Jesus as your Savior and Lord, holiness as your pursuit, and God's purpose for your life as your goal. Rev. Kent Hughes remarked on the unfortunate nature of many friendships in our society: "Friendships today have fallen on hard times. Few men have good friends, much less deep friendships. Individualism, autonomy, privatization, and isolation are culturally cachet, but deep, devoted, vulnerable friendship is not. This is a great tragedy for self, family and the church, because it is in relationships that we develop into what God wants us to be." God designed individuals to live the Christian life together. We aren't alone in our pursuit to be who God wants us to be. Believe me, many wonderful, loving people are ready to help, if we are simply willing. Never forget that Jesus will be your friend, and will remain closer to you than a brother. Jonathan Edwards called Jesus, "My true and never-failing friend." Jesus will never fail or disappoint us. Instead, He will lift us up and make us better people, which is what He does as our Savior. He lives His life in us, and believe me, His life is a disciplined life. Why not ask Him to help you?

Steps Back

√ "I strongly suspect that if you are struggling with a stronghold, you also need help. Dealing with a stronghold is not only difficult, but nearly impossible to overcome alone...I have discovered that a very effective tool in my life is my weekly meeting with an accountability group."

√ "Chuck Swindoll stated, 'When I learn of someone's spiritual defection or moral fall...I ask, "Was the person accountable to anyone on a regular basis?" Without exception—without a single exception—the answer has been the same: "NO!"'" It is vitally important to gather ourselves in a group where we can regularly be accountable to each other, especially in areas where we struggle!"

Steps Into

√ Hebrews 10:25 warns, *And let us not neglect our meeting together, as some people do, but encourage one another.*

Do you understand that God created us to lean on each other as Christians? Are you part of a church? Sunday School class? Small group Bible study? Christian fellowship group? Accountability group?

√ James 5:16 teaches, *Confess your sins to each other and pray for each other so that you may be healed.*

Do you have a person or persons who you can confess to? Why or why not?

Steps Forward

√ Why do you think accountability can help us overcome our strongholds?

√ Take some time right now and identify some people whom you might ask to join you in accountability. Consider both those who can challenge you and those you can challenge. If no individuals come to mind, ask God to show you who you might join in mutual accountability.

√ Develop some questions your accountability group could ask you to help you overcome your stronghold(s).

Chapter 8

A Step Away From Temptation

'Tis one thing to be tempted, another thing to fall.
William Shakespeare

God blesses those who patiently endure testing and
temptation. Afterward they will receive the crown of
life that God has promised to those who love him.
James 1:12

The Devil doesn't like it when we fully submit our lives
to the Lordship of Jesus Christ. He will attack us every
step of the way. F. C. Harcourt's poem reminds us of this
truth when it says the Devil "dogs the steps by tailing the
saints and digging a pit for his feet." This experience has
certainly been a reality for me over the previous months. The
Devil will not allow us to attempt any Godly change uncon-
tested. The Lord asked Satan in Job 1:8, *Have you noticed*
my servant Job? He is the finest man in all the earth. He is

blameless—a man of complete integrity. He fears God and stays away from evil.

Satan quickly noticed Job, and he has been considering God's saints ever since. I think Satan constantly considers how he can destroy us. He gave up his lofty position of serving God, and he relentlessly tries to prevent us from serving God as well. This is why he tirelessly works by attacking us with strongholds. Charles Spurgeon said, "It astounds Satan that any of us would ever want to be faithful to God." The Devil wants us to disappoint God, just as he did. If we choose otherwise, Satan will fight us throughout the entire process. You won't have to go looking for the Devil. If he found Jesus and tempted Him, believe me, he will find you. It is only in Christ that we can possibly endure what Satan will throw at us. Indeed, resisting Satan's temptations are difficult. I promise you, the Devil will give you many opportunities to come back under the grip of your stronghold.

I heard about a little boy who had spent the whole month of September stealing apples. He became convicted and told the Lord he was going to stop. One day, an apple farmer who knew what the boy had been doing saw him sitting under one of his apple trees. He went over to him and asked, "Son, are you trying to steal another one of my apples?" The boy replied, "No sir, I am trying <u>not</u> to." The Devil will make sure that the path back to our stronghold is both alluring and easy, while the path away from our stronghold is challenging. If you are like me, then you know this struggle well, but I have good news for you. We don't have to turn back to our stronghold if we will allow God to help us. I am reminded again of 1 Corinthians 10:13, *The temptations in your life are no different from what others experience. And God is faithful. He will not allow the temptation to be more than you can stand. When you are tempted, he <u>will show you a way out</u> so that you can endure.*

I want to share with you some observations that I have made concerning how the Devil works and how Christians truly have the power in Jesus Christ to stand against him. The first truth we must realize is that the Devil is a defeated foe. The Bible says in Colossians 2:14-15, *He canceled the record of the charges against us and took it away by nailing it to the cross. 15 In this way, he disarmed the spiritual rulers and authorities. He shamed them publicly by his victory over them on the cross.* Not only is the Devil a defeated foe, but one day he will be destroyed when he is cast into the "lake of fire." Until this happens, we should not be ignorant of the Devil's ways. 2 Corinthians 2:11 tells us to be mindful of the Devil *so that Satan will not outsmart us. For we are familiar with his evil schemes.*

We can't afford to be ignorant of the Devil because he will try to take advantage of us. For many years, I lived in ignorance and rebellion concerning what God's Word had to say about the care of my body. I think the Devil laughed at my rebellion and foolishness along my way to the buffet. He loves to attack our weakness and ignorance at our greatest point of rebellion. My Grandfather Brown used to preach that Jesus "cuts across our point of rebellion" to help us. I agree, but I also know that if the Devil wants to defeat us, he will tempt us at our greatest point of rebellion. For me, this point was my habit of eating all I wanted (and usually more) and exercising little (or none whatsoever).

Hebrews 4:15 teaches us a wonderful truth about Jesus. *This High Priest of ours understands our weaknesses, for he faced all of the same testings we do, yet he did not sin.* Do you know that Jesus was tempted by the Devil in every way we now experience, yet He did not sin? Because of this reality, in Jesus, we can experience victory. It's hard to imagine, but I believe that just as we are tempted, Jesus was also tempted:

- To overeat
- To lust
- To lose His temper
- To be lazy
- To steal
- To be selfish
- To become like the world
- To listen to the Devil
- To be prideful
- To step outside the boundaries of God's will

<u>BUT</u>, unlike us, Jesus never surrendered to temptation. This is what makes Him our perfect Savior. If we allow Him, Jesus will deliver us from our temptations. Jesus taught us to pray, "Lead us not into temptation but deliver us from evil." I believe Jesus will do the very thing for which He taught us to pray. It shouldn't surprise us that the Devil harasses us so often with temptations. The Devil genuinely wants our souls, but if we are children of God, he cannot have them. Our souls are secure and on their way to Heaven. Therefore, the only avenue the Devil has left to try and destroy us is to tempt us to become bogged down in a sinful stronghold. It is through this temptation that Satan hopes to negatively affect our service for the Lord. The Devil examines us and attacks where you and I are the weakest and most vulnerable.

- It could be the "lust of the eye" – something or someone we see and desire.
- It could be the "lust of the flesh" – something we would like to do and experience.
- It could be the "pride of life" – something we want to achieve or become.

Pride, materialism, sex, greed, gluttony, dishonesty—the Devil will use any or all of it to distract and destroy us. He is constantly seeking something or someone to use against us and get us off-track. Believe me, we will always face obstacles and temptations while on earth. The Devil will try to maneuver something in this world to tempt our fleshly weakness. He will try to convince us to operate outside the boundaries of God's will. To Satan, our lives are a constant game of matching temptations to our weaknesses. The Devil is an expert at this, and he knows exactly what or who we want! To corrupt and weaken our resolve, he will apply pressure in three ways.

From the World in General

The Devil is very willing to use worldly views, or a world system of thoughts and opinions, that challenge what is written in scripture. This may also be called peer pressure. As Christians, we must understand that the will of God for our lives will contradict the world's opinion of what you and I should do. This is true in every area of our lives. The Devil has convinced most of the world to live perverted lives outside the boundaries of God's will. As you and I try to live under the Lordship of Christ, the world will constantly try to pull us in another direction. For example, let's look at my weakness of overeating. The world offers us super-sized combos and all-you-can-eat buffets. By the way, do you know what the word buffet stands for?

B-Big
U-Ugly
F-Fat
F-Folks
E-Eating
T-Together

The world is not our friend while we battle our strongholds. Adrian Rogers called the world "an external foe." By and large, the world's thinking usually runs contrary to God's Word! Don't fall into the trap of peer pressure.

From Ourselves

As I mentioned in an earlier chapter, one huge obstacle to our success is our own selfish interests. This is what the Bible also calls the works of the flesh in Galatians 5:19-21,

19 When you follow the desires of your sinful nature, the results are very clear: sexual immorality, impurity, lustful pleasures, 20 idolatry, sorcery, hostility, quarreling, jealousy, outbursts of anger, selfish ambition, dissension, division, 21 envy, drunkenness, wild parties, and other sins like these.

This obstacle is what Adrian Rogers calls "our predisposition to sin." We need to continually be reminded that even if we are a Christian, our "old self" within us will always want to do the wrong thing. This "old nature" must die daily. We must say no to its desires. This is a daily discipline of self that Rogers described as an "internal foe."

I was my own worst enemy when it came to overeating. If I was not careful, I could polish off a bag of chocolate chip cookies before I would even realize it. I have actually eaten the better part of a dozen donuts (all but one) without taking a breath. I still fight temptations from within, and you will as well. It's our nature – our fallen nature. We must come to the understanding that many of our temptations to sin come from within us. We need to remind ourselves of this truth every day. I might say the Devil tempts me to turn around and follow a Little Debbie truck to its next stop. And while he may, I am convinced it was my idea to catch up with the truck and buy a box of oatmeal cream cakes. One day, we may be surprised to discover how many of our sins were a result of our own ideas! I had to come to the place where I stopped blaming everyone else, and admitted that I was the major problem. I was a glutton! I am ashamed to admit this fact to you and God, but it was an obvious truth!

From the Devil

Thirdly, we must understand that the Devil plays a role in our weaknesses. Many people don't even believe there is actually a literal Devil. Others laugh at the idea or make jokes about him. Do you believe in the Devil? He is real. In a sermon, I once asked why we always represent the Devil as a caricature in red with a pitch fork and black hair. I went on to ask if anyone had ever seen a Devil with blond hair. Three men in the congregation raised their hands that morning, saying they had! The Devil may be many things, but he is not a joke. He is an enemy of God and anyone who loves God. His name is Lucifer, and he has a plan to sabotage your life. He hopes to accomplish this plan through sinful strongholds in your life.

Throughout my life, Satan has been encouraging me to overeat and not exercise. The Devil gladly uses anything to enslave us, making us less than God wants us to be. The Devil loves to attack our bodies. When he does this, it usually isn't hard to notice, as sins committed with the body are obvious. Examine a glutton, murderer, thief, drunk, drug addict, and adulterer—their sins are obvious. Although the physical sins may be obvious, when the Devil is working on our mind, these sins do not manifest themselves quite as easily. It's easier to hide our thinking and emotions than our actions. We pretend and put up a facade. Others may not even know our secret battles. I am sure that some reading this book suffer with a secret sinful stronghold. Is this you?

We cannot overlook the fact that the Devil likes to attack us in our spiritual life. He attacks and undermines our walk with God. He discourages discipline, devotion, faithfulness, dedication and spiritual growth. The Devil will whisper lies in your ear, cast doubt on the Word of God, and even try to make you think God doesn't love you or care about you. Satan will attempt to make you feel sorry for yourself and encourage you to take comfort in a sinful pleasure that can evolve into a stronghold. People comfort themselves with alcohol, drugs, sex, or even food. It is through such strongholds that Satan tries to make us settle for less than the "abundant life" God desires to give us. The Devil offers us a way that opposes the Word of God and the Will of God. Unfortunately, we often believe his lies, and our lives become less than the healthy, holy, happy lives God has planned. Notice what Adrian Rogers wrote in *What Every Christian Ought to Know,*

> *When my body is right, I'm healthy. When my soul is right, I'm happy. When my spirit is right, I'm holy. And that's the way God intended for man to be. That's the way Adam was when he came off the assembly line. He was healthy in his body, happy in his soul, holy in his spirit; he was a whole person.*
>
> *Most of the people I know are unhealthy, unhappy, and unholy. They are out of whack because they're not what God created them to be. That's what sin has done to the human race. When the Devil comes to tempt, how does he tempt? In the body, the soul, or the spirit. Those are the only places you can be tempted because that's all there is.*

Don't let the Devil mold you into a product of worldly thinking. Don't allow the Devil to take the fleshly desires of your body and ignite them into expressions of sensual sin. Above all, do not allow the Devil to come between you and

God, and attack your faith and commitment to the Lord Jesus Christ. The Devil can't take Jesus out of your heart, but he can and will take you off of the "path of righteousness" Jesus would have you walk. If the Devil can do this in just one area of your life, this is all he needs. What area is he working on in your life? Do you realize he wants to make this area a sinful stronghold?

There is nothing wrong with the desire to be satisfied; we all experience this desire. However, the Devil will attempt to satisfy you in an unspiritual way. Do not listen to the Devil when he tempts you to look for satisfaction in places or people that do not please God. Overeating temporarily satisfied me, but left me spiritually empty. What good is a full belly with an empty soul? I am searching for satisfaction that will last. I want what God wants for me. He created me, and knows exactly what I need. Everything I do must be within His limits and boundaries. As Christians, we must all find our sole satisfaction in Jesus. I love the song that says, "Turn your eyes upon Jesus, look full in His wonderful face, and the things of earth will grow strangely dim, in the light of His glory and grace."

I am learning that you don't have to give in to temptation at any time—not even in the area of your stronghold. I have learned that I don't have to give in to the Devil. I can rebuke the Devil, and tell him to leave me alone. I want you to notice another quote from Adrian Rogers' book, *What Every Christian Ought to Know*. It comes from his chapter entitled "How to Handle Temptation." I reflect and meditate on these words frequently:

The next time the Devil gets on your trail, and you understand that the Devil is trying to drive a wedge between you and God, you don't have to take it. You can resist him. First, make sure there's no sin in your life, sin that is unconfessed and unrepented. Get your

heart clean. Then if the Devil gets on your trail, you
can say to him, "Devil, I resist you, and I rebuke you,
and I come against you in the name of Jesus Christ.
I am saved. My sin is under the blood. I have been
twice born. My body is the temple of the Holy Spirit
of God. Your back was broken at Calvary. You have
no right, you have no authority in my life. You're a
pervert. You're trespassing on my Father's property
and in the name of Jesus, be gone!" He'll flee from
you. You say, "Isn't that like praying to the Devil?"
I'm not praying to a cat when I say, "Scat!"

I was absolutely tired of the Devil defeating me in the
weak areas of my life. Do you feel the same way? Why not
join me in allowing God to do something about the shortcomings that stand in the way of your relationship with Him. My
stronghold was the sin of gluttony. I had taken a natural, God-
given appetite and perverted it! Through my own desires,
the world's influence, and the Devil's encouragement, I had
indulged in excess amounts of food and further complicated
the matter with little or no exercise. As a preacher, I quickly
pointed out the sins of others, but not my own sin of gluttony. Billy Graham wrote,

Many people guilty of gluttony are quick to condemn
others for their sins. They can readily detect a mote
of impurity in the other man but remain ignorant of
the beam of overindulgence in themselves. It is easy
for a man who surfeits and stuffs his body with need-
less delicacies to look at the man who overdrinks and
say like the Pharisee of old, "Lord, I thank Thee that
I am not as other men are: extortioners, unjust adul-
terers, or even as the Publican (Luke 18:11).

It is easy for a man who is enslaved by his stomach to condemn the man who is enslaved by alcohol. But in God's sight, "Sin is sin." God has convicted me. I have confessed it, and repented of it. Will you?

Steps Back

√ "Satan quickly noticed Job, and he has been considering God's saints ever since. I think Satan constantly considers how he can destroy us. He gave up his lofty position of serving God, and he relentlessly tries to prevent us from serving God as well. This is why he tirelessly works by attacking us with strongholds."

√ "I am learning that you don't have to give in to temptation at any time—not even in the area of your stronghold."

Steps Into

√ 1 Corinthians 10:13 emphasizes, *The temptations in your life are no different from what others experience. And God is faithful. He will not allow the temptation to be more than you can stand. When you are tempted, he <u>will show you a way out</u> so that you can endure.*

Do you realize that God has provided an escape for you with your stronghold? That you do not have to give in to temptation?

√ Hebrews 4:15 teaches, *This High Priest of ours understands our <u>weaknesses</u>, for he faced all of the same testings we do, yet he did not sin.*

Because Jesus faced the same temptations, He understands the battle you are facing. Are you willing to let Him help you out from under this stronghold?

Steps Forward

√ What are some ways that you can remove yourself from the places or areas where you are tempted the most? What "ways of escape" is Jesus providing?

√ What are some good things you can use to replace the temptation in your life?

Chapter 9

A Step Toward Devotion

A truly good book teaches me better than to read it. I must soon lay it down, and commence living on its hint. What I began by reading, I must finish by acting.

Henry David Thoreau

13...I focus on this one thing: Forgetting the past and looking forward to what lies ahead, 14 I press on to reach the end of the race and receive the Heavenly prize for which God, through Christ Jesus, is calling us.

Philippians 3:13-14

The steps in this journey have not been easy to travel. Taking control of an out-of-control area of life is certainly difficult. It is not easy to get started, and even more difficult to stay the course. The urges we fight within ourselves can be powerful, especially when we all have a desire to overindulge in something and live outside the boundaries of God's will. Clearly, in my life, overeating and lack of exercise were my most severe struggles. When I tried to address this in my life, I felt like Paul in 1 Corinthians 9:27 when he wrote that he had to "beat his body into submission." As with any stronghold, I knew I would have to discipline myself back within the boundaries of what God's Word teaches about physical health.

These past months have been an eye opening (and mouth closing) experience for me as I realized how concerned God is with my body. Bill Hybels spoke truly when he said, "Most Christians who are outraged by some sins against the body (such as sexual immorality) seem to be amazingly blind to a far more common sin (gluttony) against the body." How could I let myself be such a poor steward of something so wonderful that God has given me? How could I act with such ignorance and rebellion? I came to a clearer understanding of the following:

- After I was saved, my body didn't belong to me anymore.
- God wanted me to use my body to honor him.
- I had a body which housed the Holy Spirit.
- I had a body for which I was responsible, and my discipline was an act of worship. (Romans 12:1)

For years I offered the Lord an out of shape, undisciplined, unexercised, unkempt, overweight body that stood in the pulpit and preached. I am so disappointed in myself! Doesn't God deserve better from me? Yes, and I plan to spend the rest of my life giving Him a better, healthier me. Now, don't misunderstand, I am not on some stroll of vanity here. One of my dear senior saints heard someone say, "Our preacher is looking pretty good." She remarked, "Our preacher looks better, but I don't know if he will ever look pretty or good!" I agree with her, and besides, this isn't what is most important to me. What's most important is how I feel. Physically, I feel exceptionally healthier and more alert. Spiritually, I know I am being obedient to what God has asked me to do. Unless God deems otherwise, I know I am going to live a longer, healthier life.

We have to know that trying is not enough! Millions of people through the centuries have attempted to correct their problems, only to fail and revert back to the same bad habits. I think this is especially true in the area of weight loss, where alarming statistics show that most people gain their lost weight back within a year. Someone asked me how I felt being down to around 200 pounds. I told them I didn't know yet because I had only been at this weight for about 15 minutes! Can I stay with this? Can you and I really reach a goal and stick with it? Can we really keep weight off or our stronghold suppressed? Yes! And in this chapter, I want to emphasize four crucially important ingredients to help you stay on a course of correcting your stronghold for the rest of your life. They are <u>discipline, patience, perseverance</u> and <u>wisdom.</u>

Without a doubt, discipline will be the key to success, but patience and perseverance are increasingly important for continued success. And, wisdom provides the necessary instruction as we apply ourselves to defeating strongholds. Someone said, "The distance between intention and reality is too often littered with frustration and failure." How can we keep ourselves from being so frustrated that we give up? How can we be successful in our attempt to make it work this time? We must apply each of these ingredients.

Discipline

I have had to deny myself several things to succeed, but isn't the Christian life one of denial? Recall Jesus' words in Matthew 16:24, *Then Jesus said to his disciples, "If anyone would come after me, he must deny himself and take up his cross and follow me.* What God wants us to do is deny ourselves the things that hinder us from being all He wants us to be. I have been denying myself an excessive amount of food. I deny myself additional hours sleep in the morning, making myself get up and exercise. This led to the denial of a T.V. program at night because I had to make up for an hour of lost sleep. It's really been a choice of deciding what is most important to me—God's will or my way of doing things? Jerry Bridges describes biblical self-control when he says, "It's primarily to moderate the gratification of our desires and appetites." Believe me, <u>moderation</u> has been the key. Self-control carries with it the idea of being able to make sound judgments concerning an area. One of my favorite stories in the Bible is found in Luke 10: 38 – 42.

38 As Jesus and the disciples continued on their way to Jerusalem, they came to a certain village where a woman named Martha welcomed him into her home. 39 Her sister, Mary, sat at the Lord's feet, listening to what he taught. 40 But Martha was distracted by the big dinner she was preparing. She came to Jesus and said, "Lord, doesn't it seem unfair to you that my sister just sits here while I do all the work? Tell her to come and help me." 41 But the Lord said to her, "My dear Martha, you are worried and upset over all these details! 42 There is only <u>one thing</u> worth being concerned about. Mary has discovered it and it will not be taken away from her."

It shouldn't surprise you that one of my favorite stories would be about a woman cooking a big dinner in the kitchen (that's my kind of woman)! As you read this, you will see that there was a point where Mary left Martha in the kitchen and sat at the feet of Jesus. Martha became upset and told Jesus this was unfair because she needed help in the kitchen. Surely some of you ladies can relate to this – Amen? Interestingly, Jesus didn't rebuke Mary, but instead told Martha that Mary had learned what was truly important. Mary discerned what she *should* be doing. What a tremendous thing to have Jesus say about a person! Can He say that about you or me? Have we really learned what's most important in our lives? This knowledge will only come about with an eternal mindset and an attitude of self-denial, living our lives solely for Jesus Christ. Living life to the fullest is sitting at the feet of Jesus and knowing what He wants in each area of our lives. This is when we begin to experience the abundant life! It is especially meaningful and life-changing in the areas of our strongholds. Having a right relationship with Jesus will enable us to distinguish right from wrong, good from evil, and worst from best. Sometimes it's even a matter of distinguishing between the good and the best! Mary chose what was best in her relationship with Christ, and that's what I want to choose in every area of my life: the best. I want to make the right decision and have discernment in each area of my life, including my health.

Patience

This will not be easy. Believe me, I know! Our strongholds will not be fixed overnight. You can't put your stronghold in the microwave for 20 seconds and make it go away. Getting out from underneath the mastery of a stronghold takes time and patience. Paul encouraged us in Colossians 3:12, *Since God chose you to be the holy people he loves,* *you must clothe yourselves with tenderhearted mercy, kindness, humility, gentleness, and <u>patience</u>.*

The American Heritage dictionary defines patience as "the quality of enduring pain, hardship, provocation, or annoyances with calmness." In the Bible, it appears that patience is more often associated with having patience with people (even ourselves), conditions, circumstances, and purposes. If you and I are to make this journey successfully, we must take many steps with enduring patience. James 1:12 teaches, *God blesses those who patiently endure testing and temptation. Afterward they will receive the crown of life that God has promised to those who love him.* I am learning to daily <u>wait</u> on Him. The Psalmist described it this way in 40:1-2, *I waited patiently for the Lord to help me, and he turned to me and heard my cry. 2 He lifted me out of the pit of despair, out of the mud and the mire. He set my feet on solid ground and steadied me as I walked along.*

Anything worthwhile takes time and patience. Try not to think about overcoming your stronghold in terms of the number of days and weeks it might take, but by committing to do this for the rest of your life. It's a lifestyle change. True repentance carries with it the military phrase, "About face!" You literally reverse your course. It's not a temporary turn, but a permanent change. Addressing your stronghold with a temporary mindset will only lead to failure. I am not promising you perfect success. This won't happen until we arrive in Heaven. Instead, what I am advocating is daily discipline and a lifestyle change. In other words, not only will I address this stronghold today, but I will address this stronghold for the rest of my life. Obviously, addressing our strongholds will take an enormous amount of discipline, patience, and perseverance. You need to ask the Lord to give you patience to stay the course of correction. Robert Cook said, "Patience comes from two Greek words, meaning stay under and not always bobbing up." God doesn't want us to quit. The Bible says much about being faithful and finishing what God asks of us. Jesus taught in parables about His coming at the end of time to review our progress in accomplishing what He asked us to do. Jesus wants us to stay the course to finish all He has asked.

Perseverance

As I have walked this journey, my patience has been tested, but it has also matured. I wondered at times if I could stay the course, or if I would ever succeed. I grew frustrated when I didn't see progress as quickly as I had hoped. Couldn't I just take a pill or a shot and have the whole problem go away? I was hoping for a quick fix. Isn't this the world's solution? God constantly reminded me that this journey is not a sprint, but a marathon. True abundant living involves a consistent healthy lifestyle—both spiritually and physically. I am taking one day at a time, and I am learning to make right choices and asking God to help me make wise decisions. In this process, I have realized that weight loss really couldn't be my goal and suppressing a stronghold shouldn't be my main focus. My goal is to follow Jesus faithfully each day. The weight loss and a healthier body are simply a product of pursuing this goal. Matthew 6:33 reminds us, *Seek the Kingdom of God above all else, and live righteously, and he will give you everything you need.*

Mark Driscoll said, "If we truly put our eyes on Jesus, the rest of you can't stay the same." God began teaching me that He desired consistency, continuance, courage, and no compromise in my commitment. This was not some 12 week plan. How long would this take? The answer is the rest of my life. Many effective programs have taught alcoholics to admit they would suffer with this tendency the rest of their lives. I think this is also true with any stronghold. I still experience this with my desire to overeat and my temptation not to exercise. I suspect it's true with your stronghold as well. Do I ever feel like giving up? The answer is yes. Like you, I am human and I may sometimes want to give in. I ask God each day to prevent me from giving up or interrupting the progress I am making. It takes perseverance with continued confession and repentance. If I slip up, I try again. We aren't talking about sinless perfection, but a continued effort to be obedient. I have been encouraged by the words of Alexander Maclaren, "No matter how gifted a man may be he will be a failure if he has not learned the secret of dogged persistence in often unwelcomed toil." I am convinced those words sum up the perseverance God demands for defeating a stronghold. This is a long, slow process. You can grow a pine tree in just a few months, but it takes years to develop an oak. I want to be "oak" solid for the Lord. I love this little poem:

When you are discouraged
And feeling a little blue,
Take a look at a mighty oak
And see what a <u>nut</u> can do.

I know what some of you are thinking, and you aren't the first person to think of me as a nut. They say here in the mountains that it will be a bad winter if there are a lot of <u>plump</u> acorns. Looking at me last winter, we needed to get ready for a lot of snow! I was certainly plump. If I am going to be thought of as a "nut" at least let it be a chocolate covered nut (Go ahead and make that double-dipped)!

A big oak tree is nothing but the full development and perfection of an acorn (not necessarily a plump one). Now, I am not calling you a "nut," even though I don't mind people referring to me as one. The point I want to make is that it takes time and patience to grow and succeed, or in my case to lose and succeed. A.W. Tozer said the Christian "dies so he can live, he forsakes in order to have, he goes down in order to get up, he empties himself in order to be full." I am asking the Lord to help me practice this each day.

God has shown me to actively do the right things each day while I wait to learn all He wants to do in my life. Hebrews 6:12 teaches, *Then you will not become spiritually dull and indifferent. Instead, you will follow the example of those who are going to inherit God's promises because of their <u>faith</u> and <u>endurance</u>.* If I experience struggles along the way, I am trying to endure them with perseverance. Do you realize that <u>longsuffering</u>, <u>forbearance</u>, <u>endurance</u>, and <u>perseverance</u> are all fruit of the Spirit? *But what happens when we live God's way? He brings gifts into our lives, much the same way that fruit appears in an orchard—things like affection for others, exuberance about life, serenity. We develop a <u>willingness to stick with things.</u>"* Galatians 5:22 (The Message)

No matter what obstacle, resistance or adversity comes my way, I am asking the Lord for perseverance to carry on with what He has asked me to do. His commands are clear, and my obedience is to be prompt and continual. I have made up my mind that I will not quit. The words of the poem from an unknown author entitled "The Race" have grown to be significant to me on my journey for abundant life.

Defeat! He lay there silently, a tear dropped from his eye.
"There's no sense running anymore –
three strikes, I'm out – why try?"
The will to rise had disappeared, all hope had fled away,
So far behind, so error prone, closer all the way.
"I've lost, so what's the use," he thought,
"I'll live with my disgrace."
But then he thought about his dad who
soon he'd have to face.
"Get up," an echo sounded low,
"Get up and take your place.
You were not meant for failure here,

so get up and win the race."
With borrowed will, "Get up," it said
"You haven't lost at all,
For winning is not more than this –
to rise each time you fall."
So up he rose to win once more, and with a new commit,
He resolved that win or lose, at least he wouldn't quit.
So far behind the others now, the most he'd ever been,
Still he gave it all he had and ran as though to win.
Three times he'd fallen stumbling,
three times he rose again,
Too far behind to hope to win, he still ran to the end.
They cheered the winning runner as he crossed first place,
Head high and proud and happy; no falling, no disgrace.
But when the fallen youngster crossed the line, last place,
The crowd gave him the greater cheer for
finishing the race.
And even though he came in last,
with head bowed low, unproud;
You would have thought he won the race,
to listen to the crowd.
And to his dad he sadly said, "I didn't do so well."
"To me, you won," his father said.
"You rose each time you fell,"
And now when things seem dark and hard
and difficult to face,
The memory of that little boy helps in my race.
For all of life is like that race,
with ups and downs and all,
And all you have to do to win – is rise each time you fall.
"Quit! Give up, you're beaten," they still shout in my face.
But another voice within me says,
"Get up and win that race."

I find myself praying, "Lord, help me not to quit!"

Wisdom

In addition to my desire for discipline, patience, and perseverance, I have also requested that God grant me wisdom. James 1:5 instructs, *If you need wisdom, ask our generous God, and he will give it to you. He will not rebuke you for asking.* I have been asking God each day for guidance. In this quest to overcome my stronghold, I have been amazed at how much excellent information exists in the areas of exercise, nutrition, breathing, stretching, mindset, strongholds, temptation, spiritual warfare, and many other issues we face. I have asked God to use these resources to help me on my journey. Of course, my best source of information is the Bible. I am praying that God would daily transform me into the likeness of His Son, Jesus.

I am convinced that one common denominator in every individual's battle with a stronghold is a lack of daily Bible reading and prayer. You may be asking why, as a pastor, this would be my problem. Surely, as a pastor, I would regularly study the Bible and pray. You are right! I spend the first half of nearly every day in my study preparing for my sermons and praying. However, I have come to realize that I need time in Bible study that doesn't involve sermon preparation. I need to daily read God's Word, allowing Him to speak to my own life. I need to grow personally. There is no substitute for consistent daily Bible reading and letting God's Word speak to us in a personal way. I suggest you take this time studying the Bible early in the morning so that you are able to meditate on what you have read throughout the day. This gives the Holy Spirit an opportunity to further impress these truths on our hearts, minds, and bodies. It will also keep these truths fresh in our mind for practical application as circumstances unfold each day. Do you know that you can easily read the entire Bible within a couple of years? There are several well-planned programs to read the whole Bible within even one year. Everything God desires us to know is right inside the covers of His Holy Word. Read it daily with the purpose of applying it to your life. Like me, you will be amazed at how it will personally speak to you. With consistent daily reading, I am astounded at how God says exactly what I need each day.

Steps Back

√ "Without a doubt, discipline will be the key to success, but patience and perseverance are increasingly important for continued success. And, wisdom provides the necessary instruction as we apply ourselves to defeating strongholds."

√ "In this quest to overcome my stronghold, I have been amazed at how much excellent information exists in the areas of exercise, nutrition, breathing, stretching, mindset, strongholds, temptation, spiritual warfare, and many other issues we face. I have asked God to use these resources to help me on my journey. Of course, my best source of information is the Bible. I am praying that God would daily transform me into the likeness of His Son, Jesus."

Steps Into

√ In Philippians 3:13-14 Paul challenges, *13...I focus on this one thing: Forgetting the past and looking forward to what lies ahead, 14 I press on to reach the end of the race and receive the Heavenly prize for which God, through Christ Jesus, is calling us.*

Where is your focus: your past defeats or your future reward? The beginning and end of devotion must be Christ Himself. Is He your primary goal?

√ Galatians 5:22 encourages, *But what happens when we live God's way? He brings gifts into our lives, much the same way that fruit appears in an orchard—things like affection for others, exuberance about life, serenity. We develop a willingness to stick with things." (The Message)*

Are you developing "a willingness to stick with things" in your battle to be free from sinful strongholds? Are you seeing evidence of God's work in your life?

Steps Forward

√ Honestly evaluate your relationship with God. Are you spending time in His Word every day? Are you

praying and depending on Him to give you strength
to overcome your stronghold(s)?

√ How can discipline, patience, perseverance, and
   wisdom aid you in experiencing victory in your
   Christian walk?

√ If you are willing, take some time to write an honest
   prayer to God acknowledging your weaknesses and
   strongholds, submitting to His Lordship, and asking
   Him to empower you to overcome.

Conclusion

Life is a series of changes that create challenges. And if we are going to make it we have to grow. When we stop growing, we stop living and start existing. There is no growth without challenge and there is no challenge without change. If you really want to grow, then be willing to change.
Warren Wiersbe

So all of us who have had that veil removed can see and reflect the glory of the Lord. And the Lord—who is the Spirit—makes us more and more like him as we are changed into his glorious image.
2 Corinthians 3:18

For many of us, the real issue in overcoming our stronghold is getting started. Don't you think you have been a slave to your stronghold long enough? I certainly felt that way. Enough is enough! As the Bible says, "The night is far spent and the day is at hand." It's time to do something about our strongholds. The issue isn't God's ability, but our willingness. Would you ask God to make you willing? Like the old preachers used to say, "Even if you aren't willing right now, would you at least pray a prayer asking God to convict you and <u>make you willing</u>?" The determination of our will is an essential step to success. Years ago, I remember hearing one of my favorite preachers, Ron Dunn, preaching on Romans 12:1,

> *And so, dear brothers and sisters, I plead with you to give your bodies to God because of all he has done for you. Let them be a living and holy sacrifice—the kind he will find acceptable. This is truly the way to worship him.*

He said, "The presenting of your bodies in that verse is a determination of your will. It is coming to the place where you and I say, 'Alright Lord, I mean business and to prove it I am presenting my body and all that resides in it (mind, soul, spirit, emotions) to your Lordship.'" We should not only do this today, but strive to do it daily for the rest of our lives. Only when we present ourselves to God in this way will we experience the transformation and revelation of God's plan for our lives found in Romans 12:2:

> *Don't copy the behavior and customs of this world, but let God <u>transform</u> you into a new person by changing the way you think. Then you will learn to know God's will for you, which is good and pleasing and perfect.*

Isn't this our purpose for living?

- To present our whole beings to God.
- To be changed into His likeness.

- To know His good, perfect, and acceptable will for our lives.

I long for this! As I have journeyed these last months in this direction, I have enjoyed the abundant life Jesus described in John 10:10, *The thief's purpose is to steal and kill and destroy. My purpose is to give them a rich and satisfying life.* What God wants for me is so much better. It is such a sweet and rewarding experience. I have commented to others that my weight loss has been worth it just to physically feel so much better. However, I have discovered that it has been worth so much more to feel better spiritually. God has helped me lift an estimated 100 pound stronghold off of my shoulders (or should I say my feet?). Strongholds aren't only difficult, but they are heavy. Aren't you tired of lugging yours around? Hasn't your stronghold defeated you long enough? Why not let this time be different and allow God to lead you to do something about it? I believe those of you reading this book are like me—you also have a serious decision to make. You may be at a critical time in your life. Making the wrong decision will only cost you more heartache and defeat. And, if you make the wrong decision, you may also continue to hurt others, especially those who love you and need you. At this point, the lack of a disciplined decision may lead to an early grave. Are you willing to address your stronghold? F.W. Boreham said, "We make our decision, and then our decisions turn around and make us." If you make no decision at all, you actually make a decision not to address your stronghold. If you wait too long to decide, you may forfeit this opportunity given to you.

I wonder where you are in your spiritual walk with Christ. Has God patiently waited on you? Has He lovingly convicted and shown you a clear course of correction? Have you ever wondered just how long God will tolerate your lack of discipline and indecision? There is a passage of scripture God has used several times in my life to grab my attention and help me gain perspective. Luke 13:6-9 teaches this parable,

> *6 Then Jesus told this story: "A man planted a fig tree in his garden and came again and again to see if there was any fruit on it, but he was always disappointed. 7 Finally, he said to his gardener, 'I've waited three years, and there hasn't been a single fig! Cut it down. It's just taking up space in the garden.' 8 "The gardener answered, 'Sir, give it one more chance. Leave it another year, and I'll give it special attention and plenty of fertilizer. 9 If we get figs next year, fine. If not, then you can cut it down.'"*

The owner of the garden was frustrated because the fig tree wouldn't produce figs. Was that an unreasonable expectation on his part? Isn't the purpose of any fig tree in existence to produce figs? Of course, the answer is yes, and you don't even have to hold a degree in "figology" to come to this conclusion. It was a simple, reasonable expectation. The owner was ready to cut the fig tree down. It had been given every opportunity for years to produce. To further understand the owner's disappointment in the fig tree, I want you to notice several things. The fig tree had been <u>carefully</u> planted in his garden. It wasn't growing out on a random hillside with no one to care for it and give it an opportunity to produce. It was not growing in a time of drought with no water or nourishment. It was not being rushed to produce prematurely. It was given every opportunity to produce, but still it produced nothing. The owner was ready to remove it when the gardener said, "Let's give it one more year." The gardener offered the fig tree an opportunity to change. He said he would give it attention and resources. Actually, he said he would give the tree special attention to assist it in the production of figs. I believe I have been like that fig tree. I can only speak for myself, and I will leave the rest up to you and the Holy Spirit for any personal application in your life. Personally, I believe God spoke to my heart (with an over-weight body around it) and indicated that His patience was growing thin with this fat preacher. I totally ignored a major concern and stronghold in my life. In retrospect, I realize many others were concerned about me. Recently, a lady spoke to me about my weight loss. She said that two years ago God spoke to her and told her I was sick. I replied to her, "Ma'am I wasn't sick; I was fat." Sincerely, some people do have health issues from which they suffer and can't do anything about, even if they exercise and eat properly. Only medicine or a miracle can help them. With me, it was pure laziness and a lack of discipline. I wasn't sick. I was lazy and fat. I was digging an early grave with a knife and a fork! I had no real excuse, and God was tired of my fabricated excuses. God lovingly said, "It's time to do something about this." Did He give me a year? I don't guess we will know this side of Heaven, but He certainly did impress on me to immediately act! I knew better! I was warned by my doctor, encouraged by my family, and even prayed for by my congregation. Still, I had done virtually nothing. One member even offered to pay me money for every pound I lost (I'm still open to that).

What finally got me started? It came down to God and me. While this process has involved a lot of physical exercise, it really has been a spiritual work of God in my heart and life. I have experienced a spiritual transformation with some physical results. I simply and powerfully came back to the foot of the cross of Jesus. Where I found salvation in Jesus, I also found sanctification. Where I gave Him my soul, I also gave Him my body. With brokenness, confession, and repentance I gave my stronghold to the Lord. I actually took some items in my life that represented this stronghold and laid them at the bottom of a little wooden cross in my study.

I use it as a reminder that I am serious about this commitment to God. I decided this stronghold was not more important to me than His Lordship. I asked God to free me of this stronghold and give me the guidance, strength, and patience to persevere. What a wonderful experience this has been and continues to be! I cannot help but think of the words of the old hymn,

> At the cross, at the cross
> Where I first saw the light,
> And the burden of my heart rolled away,
> It was there by faith I received my sight,
> And now I am happy all the day!

I have been daily praising the Lord and living in victory over this stronghold. I have truly been experiencing Romans 8:37, *No, despite all these things, overwhelming victory is ours through Christ, who loved us.* At least in this area of my life, I have been experiencing the victorious Christian life. This is a goal realized, and the victory is won!

You may be wondering what I am up to these days with my slimmer, stronger, healthier self. Well, I have been meditating on that verse in Romans 8:37. The problem is, God continues to show me the word "things" in that verse. It is plural. I can have victory in all areas, in all things. While this book has been about one "thing" and about one problem in my life, God didn't stop with that. He has been pointing out some other "things" I need to work on. At the beginning of this book, do you remember the story about the little girl who asked me, "Preacher, what all sins have you been committing?" Let me confess, there are more "things" (sins), and God has been convicting me of all of them. You may ask what they are. I have told you one big one. Isn't that enough? Perhaps with a little more conviction, I might reveal a few others. Believe me, God is truly working on me "in all things." I have been confessing these sins to God. While I was writing this chapter, a man asked, "Preacher, are you ready for a revival, a spiritual awakening?" I told him "Yes!" He said, "Well I see one happening in you!" The old preachers used to say, "If you want to have revival, get in the altar and draw a circle around yourself. Then ask God to help the person in the circle." I have done this, and God continues to help me. As I give Him more of my life, I notice my circle isn't as big as it used to be! I hope you see more of Him and less of me. Remember the words of John the Baptist, "I must decrease and He must increase." That's exactly what God wants in me.

Do you know how I want to live the rest of my life? Just following Jesus! Do you remember in John 21 when Jesus was helping Peter get back on the right track? Jesus told Peter to "focus on his own devotion, dedication, and purpose in life." Peter, like many of us, looked around and said, "Well what about John over there?" Jesus responded, "Don't worry about John and what he should or shouldn't do...You follow Me!" This is the point I have come to. Whatever God wants you to do is between you and Him. I know what He wants me to do, and I am doing it. I can't make you do anything, nor would I try. If God leads you, I would be more than pleased to have you join me on this journey. I know God is able to help you—are you willing to let Him help? He is the Potter, and we are the clay. He not only wants to mold us but perhaps sometimes even trim us up! Are you willing to ask God what He wants to do in your life? If your answer is yes, then get ready for a journey that will change your life.

23 Now may the God of peace make you holy in every way, and may your whole spirit and soul and body be kept blameless until our Lord Jesus Christ comes again.
1 Thessalonians 5:23

6 And I am certain that God, who began the good work within you, will continue his work until it is finally finished on the day when Christ Jesus returns.
Philippians 1:6

List of References

Introduction
A. W. Tozer. *The Pursuit of God*. Wingspread Publishers, 2000.

Chapter 1
Step Toward Honesty
Paul Lee Tan. *Encyclopedia of 7700 Illustrations*. Assurance Publishers, 1984.
Patrick Morley. *The Man in the Mirror*. Zondervan Publishers, 1997.

Chapter 2
Step Toward Evaluation
Bill Hybels. *Honest to God?* Zondervan Publishers, 1990.

Chapter 3
Step Toward Identity
Mrs. Charles E. Cowman. *Streams in the Desert*. Zondervan Publishers, 1999.
Jack Taylor. *The Key to Triumphant Living*. Seedsowers Publishers, 1996.
Hannah Whitall Smith. *The Christian's Secret of a Happy Life*. Fleming H. Revell, 1952.

Jerry Bridges. *The Pursuit of Holiness*. NavPress, 2006.
Ruth Harms Calkin. *Tell Me Again, Lord, I Forget*. Tyndale House Publishers, 1986.

Chapter 4
Step Toward His Lordship
Chuck Colson. *Loving God*. Zondervan Publishers, 1997.

Chapter 5
Step Toward Purity
The Biblical Recorder. 19 July 2008.

Chapter 6
Step Toward Discipline
The Biblical Recorder. 19 July 2008.
Sam Varner. *Slimmer, Younger, Stronger*. 3d Ed. Faith Printing Company, 2005.

Chapter 7
Step Toward Accountability
Patrick Morley. *The Man in the Mirror*.

Chapter 8
Step Away From Temptation
Adrian Rogers. *What Every Christian Ought to Know*. Broadman and Holman Publishers, 2005.
Billy Graham. *The 7 Deadly Sins*. Zondervan Publishers, 1955.

9 781607 913603